Buying Security:
Iran Under the Monarchy

Studies in International Politics

Leonard Davis Institute for International Relations
The Hebrew University, Jerusalem

Buying Security: Iran Under the Monarchy, Ann Tibbitts Schulz

Africa and Israel: Relations in Perspective, Olusola Ojo

The Illusion of Deterrence: The Roosevelt Presidency and the Origins of the Pacific War, Abraham Ben-Zvi

Europe's Middle East Dilemma: The Quest for a Unified Stance, Ilan Greilsammer and Joseph Weiler

Dynamics of Dependence: U.S.-Israeli Relations, Gabriel Sheffer, ed.

Jordan's Palestinian Challenge, 1948-1983: A Political History, Clinton Bailey

STUDIES IN INTERNATIONAL POLITICS
LEONARD DAVIS INSTITUTE FOR INTERNATIONAL RELATIONS
THE HEBREW UNIVERSITY, JERUSALEM

Buying Security:
Iran Under the Monarchy

Ann Tibbitts Schulz

Westview Press
BOULDER, SAN FRANCISCO, & LONDON

Studies in International Politics, Leonard Davis Institute for International Relations, The Hebrew University, Jerusalem

This Westview softcover edition is printed on acid-free paper and bound in softcovers that carry the highest rating of the National Association of State Textbook Administrators, in consultation with the Association of American Publishers and the Book Manufacturers' Institute.

Published in 1989 in the United States of America by Westview Press, Inc., 5500 Central Avenue, Boulder, Colorado 80301, and in the United Kingdom by Westview Press, Inc., 13 Brunswick Centre, London WC1N 1AF, England

Library of Congress Cataloging-in-Publication Data
Schulz, Ann Tibbitts.
  Buying security: Iran under the monarchy/by Ann Tibbitts Schulz.
    p.   cm—(Studies in international politics)
  Bibliography: p.
  Includes index.
  ISBN 0-8133-7661-0
  1. Iran—Armed Forces—Appropriations and expenditures.   2. Iran—
Armed Forces—Procurement.   3. Iran—Military Policy—Economic
aspects.   4. Iran—Defenses—Economic aspects. I. Title.
II. Series: Studies in international politics (Boulder, Colo.)
UA853.I7S34   1989
338.4'3355'00955—dc20   89-32207
                                                                     CIP

Printed and bound in the United States of America

The paper used in this publication meets the requirements of the American National Standard for Permanence of Paper for Printed Library Materials Z39.48-1984.

10   9   8   7   6   5   4   3   2   1

Contents

List of Tables
and Figures

ix

FIGURES

Acknowledgments

I express my gratitude to the Swedish Agency for Research Cooperation with Developing Countries, which funded the original case study, and to Nicole Ball and Milton Leitenberg as principal investigators for the project.

The original manuscript was typed by Terry Reynolds and Karen E. Shepardson of the Word Processing Center, Clark University. I thank them for their help.

Finally, the willingness of several people to read the manuscript and to comment on it is very much appreciated, although, for political reasons, I shall not mention them by name. Many persons involved in carrying out the Shah's military and economic programs offered their time and recollections during a difficult period of their exile.

Ann Tibbitts Schulz

ONE

Introduction

In 1980, the Swedish Agency for Research Cooperation with Developing Countries (SAREC) agreed to support a project that would investigate the economic impact of military spending on developing countries. This case study is one product of that project. Interest in the relationship between arms and economic growth has mounted since the early 1970s. The first cross-national research in this area, published in 1973, was funded by the U.S. Agency for International Development.[1] Two Special Sessions on Disarmament and Development have been conducted by the United Nations and preparations for a third are under way at this writing. The U.N. also has funded several comparative research projects on military expenditures and development.[2]

Two worldwide trends help to account for the interest of public agencies in the question of military spending and its economic consequences. Since 1970, most Third World governments have chosen to increase the proportion of their budgets spent on military programs in general, and on weapons procurement in particular.[3] Over the same period, the North-South conflict over economic issues has become polarized, with the governments of neither group being willing to accept substantial responsibility for poverty and inequality.

One of the questions about the causes of continuing poverty is the relationship between government expenditures, including military spending, and economic growth. Statistics show that the military portion of government spending is indeed higher among low-income countries.[4] Not surprisingly, the question has become very politicized, and it is worthwhile to look briefly at the politics before we delve into the more academic issues.

1

From the perspective of the "North," or the industrialized countries, excessive or wasteful government spending makes an important contribution to poverty. Conservatives and liberals alike can find historical support for their political views in this explanation. From a conservative point of view, if government spending is a significant drag on economic growth, corrective measures are clearly the responsibility of the Third World governments themselves and redistributing resources from North to South will only postpone the day of political accountability for the latter. From a liberal perspective, diverting resources from the military to the civilian economy would produce higher rates of growth. According to this view, excessive military spending is a result of a kind of "political malfunctioning," a combination of corruption and the imposition of superpower competition in regional politics. From this perspective, too, a reformist solution to poverty and underdevelopment is possible, and a major restructuring of the international economic system can be avoided.

In contrast to both these perspectives, Third World leaders tend to see the controversy over military spending as a preoccupation of the industrialized countries and its reduction as an unacceptable alternative, given the security threats that they face. From their perspective, structural reforms in the international economic order are the most promising response to poverty, not cutting back on military budgets,[5] a position which is quite close to the official views of the communist governments.

The discussion of the economic impact of military spending has taken on a second, related, dimension that also bridges politics and academic research. The gravity of current levels of military *and* economic insecurity has elevated the guns-or-butter question into a controversy over the fundamentals of national security. The fundamental need for physical security as a prerequisite for economic growth is unquestioned. But the reverse—the role of economic growth in national security—is the subject of much debate.

One view of national security emphasizes a country's military capabilities and the attendant technological and industrial accoutrements of military power. Others focus on the economic foundation of national security, including human welfare as well as economic growth. From the latter perspective, military security purchased at the cost of economic growth and development may actually have the effect of reducing national security in the long term.

The United States' foreign assistance policies have sought to maintain a rough balance between these two approaches. In 1983, the U.S. Commission on Security and Economic Assistance (known as the Carlucci Commission) reiterated the official position that "foreign security and economic cooperation programs are mutually-supportive and interrelated, and together constitute an essential and integral part of the foreign policy of the United States."[6]

At the policymaking level, however, conflicts between military and economic security can and do arise. First, a balance between the two is politically difficult to maintain when investment decisions are being made within the context of competition for scarce resources. Second, military expenditure and investments designed to promote economic growth and development are not necessarily "mutually-interrelated," as the commission proposed. Military technology, for example, has changed dramatically since the Second World War and most political leaders choose to purchase the most advanced weapons available. However, nonmilitary investment projects involving similar technologies may not produce sustained economic growth in the civilian sector, particularly in the less industrial countries. There is no doubt that the question of how military expenditures and economic performance are related is a significant one and that the answers to this question will require extensive research.

FINDING AN ECONOMIC PARADIGM

This study looks at trends in military expenditures in Iran during, approximately, the three decades preceding the Islamic revolution of 1979 and their impact on economic growth and development. The interaction between military expenditures and the civilian sector is complex in any economy. Several different approaches to understanding this interaction have been taken in earlier research. One has been to use econometric analysis to determine whether or not aggregate military expenditures bear an empirical relationship to aggregate growth and/or investment rates over time or to indicators of development, like education and health.[7] Econometric analysis depends on valid data and a solid theoretical foundation to ensure the inclusion of all relevant variables in the analysis. Emile Benoit, for example, found that capital inflows were an important intervening link between military expenditures and growth.

Other analysts look at military spending and civilian growth more as discrete alternatives and discuss the alternatives in terms of the political and economic opportunity costs attached to each.[8] Opportunity cost studies have usually used less complex data analysis than have econometric studies, although there is no technical reason for doing so. These studies have been policy oriented, and have tended to emphasize the nonmilitary uses of military dollars.

Looking beyond the empirical relationship between highly aggregated spending and growth figures, other economists have identified possible contributions to economic growth that could be made by military spending. The list of benefits includes (1) raising aggregate demand by increasing wages and employment; (2) creating infrastructure that would provide external economies to civilian production; (3) initiating and/or subsidizing the production of intermediate and capital goods so as to increase productivity in civilian industries; and (4) training workers to use new technologies. In addition, political sociologists have hypothesized that military service fosters nationalism, discipline, and innovative attitudes that improve labor productivity.[9]

The propositions that military spending stimulates economic growth in these ways have been questioned by economists who have focused on the unique attributes of less industrial countries.[10] Among other issues, researchers have addressed the distinction between an economy's ability to produce new technologies versus grafting on imported military technology,[11] the relationship between military technology and the direction of growth in civilian industry and agriculture,[12] and the characteristics of "infant military industries" in less industrial countries.[13]

Much of the research on military spending and growth, including this study, has proceeded in a somewhat ad hoc manner. The absence of a tight theoretical grounding is a symptom of the lack of consensus among social scientists on how growth and development actually take place. To make this point, the author of a 1978 article on Iranian military spending contrasts the alternative theories of "balanced growth" and "the big push."[14] If balanced growth were the most significant consideration, then the impact of military spending on the distribution of income and on the development of human resources would be of greatest importance. On the other hand, adherents of the "big push" theory argue that growth in a leading sector will eventually stimulate a positive response from other sectors. Therefore, the impact of military spending would be assessed on the basis of whether or not it contributed, for example, to rapid change in industrial technology.

Second, unidentified intervening variables may explain the empirical relationships found to exist between military spending and growth, variables that may not be quantifiable themselves. Benoit concluded that foreign capital inflows helped to explain the positive relationship and that investment capacity might also be a factor. The nonquantifiable variables that potentially influence the impact of military spending on growth could include political instability, conflict between various economic groups, and conflict over military security goals. Finally, there is the difficulty of explaining what causality is operating. A political perspective could suggest that economic growth simply provides the wherewithal for governments to increase military spending.

Nevertheless, much can be learned about the economics of military spending even though we do not all agree about how growth takes place and despite our inability to measure all the variables that affect growth. All three approaches that have been used to understand the impact of military spending—aggregate, intermediate sector, and opportunity cost analysis—can be used to gain a balanced view of military spending and growth. This study draws on each. It is useful, when evaluating analytical approaches, to bear in mind the fact that a primary goal of research on military spending and growth is to clarify policy alternatives. The issues involve incremental decisions, that is, trying to locate the most costly aspects of military spending and implementing compensatory economic policies and/or marginal revisions in military budget categories. Realistically, the precision of research results is not as significant in determining policy as is the politics of military budget-making.

WHAT THIS STUDY INCLUDES

Because military spending is a policy issue, the starting place for this study is military security policy, which establishes guidelines for military spending decisions. Chapter 2 discusses the evolution of the Shah's ideas about how to achieve military security. The remainder of the book considers the financial costs of translating these ideas into policy (Chapters 3-5), and the influence of security policy on public sector planning and private sector performance (Chapters 6-9). The relationship between the Iranian government's military spending and improving technology and the production of capital goods is discussed in the context of arms industries (Chapter 4) and the changes occurring in specific sectors of the economy (Chapters 7-9). How military spending affects demand, employment, training, and worker attitudes is taken up in Chapter 9.

The research draws on economic and government budget data, secondary sources of information about politics, planning, and investment policies, and the firsthand observations of former military officers, planning officials, and industrialists. The methodological problems that arise when using quantitative, aggregate data to determine empirical relationships between military spending and growth and development have been discussed in useful detail in other publications.[15] From the perspective of our case study, we can add to the methodological critiques the observation that economic statistics are not very precise. This is true of statistics produced for any economy; it certainly is the case for Iran, although statistical collection and analysis improved tremendously after 1970. Therefore, conclusions based on those statistics will also be imprecise, although accurate in their general direction.

The study has drawn on political observations because such factors are likely to come into play in the relationship between military expenditures and growth: political instability, conflict among various economic actors, and specific military security situations. These factors also are important because they may help to shed light on the direction of influence or causality in quantitatively identified relationships. For example, the positive relationship that some studies have found between military expenditures and growth may best be explained in political terms as the result of governments' tendencies to spend whatever resources they have access to and the fact that those resources are more abundant in times of economic growth.

A STATE UNTO ITSELF

From the standpoint of relevance to military security and economic policy, the often hostile relations between the rulers and the ruled is one of the most salient characteristics of Iranian political history. A Dutch sociologist, C.A.O. van Nieuwenhuijze, found this phenomenon to be typical of Middle Eastern societies.[16] Descriptions of Iranian political life refer to a lack of trust which extends to the state and fosters a notable need to rely on personal ties for the apparatus of the state to function. A distance between local bureaucrats and politicians on the one hand, and the people they were to serve on the other, was equally apparent in this author's field work in Iran.

The isolation of the state in Iran was not always as pronounced as it became in the twentieth century. Previously, the state was more dependent on other institutions and groups in Iranian society and, as a consequence, rulers had to maintain a measure of political reciprocity with them. Under the nineteenth-century Qajar dynasty, the state depended on tribal leaders and provincial landowners for soldiers and taxes, and occasionally on the mosque for loans.[17] Rulers found it to their advantage to permit flexibility in some of these arrangements. For example, landowners could receive tax exemptions if they provided soldiers instead.

Other revenues came from customs levies, foreign loans, and from a variety of corrupt practices such as selling official positions in Teheran and the provinces. The Qajars also used foreign connections for military support and training. Their recourse to foreign governments and financiers was as unpopular at that time as it is in contemporary Iran and it hastened the dynasty's downfall.

In the twentieth century, the state's independence grew. Reza Shah Pahlavi (1925-1941), who had a military background, began to consolidate the armed forces as soon as he came to power. He was successful in this effort partly because he took power after a period of considerable political turmoil that took place under the last, weakened Qajar monarch. His purposefulness was a contrast to Ahmad Shah's placid immaturity, and there were few in civilian politics whose energies had not been exhausted by the previous period of revolution and continuing foreign interference with Iran's fledgling constitutional government.

The political effects of the consolidation were evident in many areas. Government military forces fought against tribal armies whose support had earlier been solicited. Discipline was imposed within the military hierarchy. Qajar soldiers had been known to stage open protests against their superiors over issues such as salaries; this was not to happen under the Pahlavis until that dynasty's last days.

The second change was the financial independence that oil revenues brought to the state. By the 1970s, oil revenues were providing three-quarters of the government's income and government investment in

the economy surpassed private investment. Without its former dependence on the population for taxes, the state's power could easily be exag-
gerated by those who controlled it. From his beginning as a young and
relatively timid ruler, Mohammed Reza Shah came to entertain the idea
of reconstructing Iran according to his own image of its potential military
power and modernity.[18]

The distance between the state and those whom it ruled was a
reality; the power of the state to transform without a political mechanism
was a potentiality. There were people who were close to the Shah and
his court. They came from important segments of the population,[19] but it
would be overstating the cohesiveness of those groups to say that those
in favor at court *represented* the groups in either a corporate or a political
sense. The Shah discouraged any political contacts other than those he
established with specific individuals.

The Shah's hope of using the state to establish Iran as a military
power and a modern society was fostered by Iran's relations with the
United States and other industrialized countries. The encouragement
and involvement of foreign advisers in both areas contributed to the be-
lief that substantial military and economic changes could be accomplished through state planning and direction. In fact, it was not unusual
for U.S. military assistance to be predicated on the initiation of social and
economic reconstruction.[20] Beginning in the early 1960s, these efforts en-
countered opposition from important segments of the population (the bazaar, clergy, and landowners) that had a stronger political base than did
the Shah.

The alliance with the United States and the negotiated reforms
left the Shah more isolated from domestic politics than before. It was
during this period that Ayatollah Khomeini's enmity toward the Pahlavis
came into the open. More broadly, demonstrations led by the bazaar and
the clergy against the reforms were ended by bringing in the military. In
1964 Abol Hassan Ebtehaj, former director of the government's planning
agency, observed the Shah's shift toward state-centered methods of governing. He told a meeting of industrialists in San Francisco that the assistance the United States was providing the Iranian government was not
stimulating economic development as much as it was moving Iran along
the path toward arbitrary rule.[21]

CONCLUSION

It was in this context, here briefly sketched, that the military buildup of the 1960s and 1970s occurred. The political distance between the state and the population not only helps to account for the specific military policies that were adopted, but also for how they were implemented and with what impact on the economy. In retrospect, U.S. policymakers involved in Iranian affairs prefer to explain the 1979 revolution as occurring because the Shah "tried to go too fast."[22]

One interpretation of Iran's political history would be that "too fast" meant that its rulers tried to stretch their influence beyond the internal political limits of state power. The willingness of government to undertake short-term risks to realize long-term collective gains is often cited as one of the advantages of state intervention in economic activities. It is an advantage that apparently applies in some situations. However, this author's interviews with economic planners indicate that these situations are likely to be ones in which the desired changes are not too far away from existing economic, social, and political constructs.[23]

Military spending has two dimensions: the financial resources spent and the process of spending them. Neither in quantity nor as a process do military spending decisions follow axiomatically from similarly clear "laws" of military security. The next three chapters look at a number of the assumptions that were made about military security and what the decisions about military spending were that grew out of these assumptions. It is hoped that this approach will promote a more flexible view of military spending. Policymakers will only evaluate their decisions if there appear to be politically feasible options.

NOTES

1. Emile Benoit, *Defense and Economic Growth in Developing Countries* (Lexington, Mass.: Lexington Books, 1973).

2. See United Nations, *Economic and Social Consequences of the Arms Race and of Military Expenditures* (New York: United Nations, 1983).

3. The arms trade increased fourfold from 1970 to 1979. Approximately seventy-five percent of the arms trade consists of transfers to the Third World. *World Armaments and Disarmament: SIPRI Yearbook 1980* (Stockholm: Almquist & Wiksell, 1980), p. 61.

4. Robert L. West, "Provision for National Security in Developing Countries," preparatory note for participants in the Conference on Development and Security in the

Third World, Fletcher School of Law and Diplomacy, Tufts University, April 12-13, 1984, mimeo, p. 10.

5. This author has taken part in discussions of military spending among U.N. First and Second Committee representatives from less industrial countries. In the discussions, most of the participants refused to consider the question of economic tradeoffs, given the security threats their countries faced. They held the position that restructuring international trade and finance was a more realistic response to their economic difficulties than military spending.

6. U.S. Commission on Security and Economic Assistance, *A Report to the Secretary of State* (Washington, D.C.: the Commission, 1983).

7. In addition to Benoit, *Defense and Economic Growth,* see R. Faini, P. Annez, and L. Taylor, "Defense Spending, Economic Structure, and Growth: Evidence Among Countries and Over Time," *Economic Development and Cultural Change* 32, 3 (April 1984): 487-498; Saadet Deger and Ron Smith, "Military Expenditure and Growth in Less Developed Countries," *Journal of Conflict Resolution* 27, 2 (June 1983): 335-363; P.C. Frederiksen and Robert E. Looney, "Defense Expenditures and Economic Growth in Developing Countries," *Armed Forces and Society* 9, 4 (Summer 1983): 633-645; David Lim, "Another Look at Growth and Defense in Less Developed Countries," *Economic Development and Cultural Change,* 31, 2 (January 1983): 377-384; Gavin Kennedy, *The Military in the Third World* (London: Duckworth, 1974).

8. Hossein Askari and Vittorio Gorbo, "Economic Implications of Military Expenditures in the Middle East," *Journal of Peace Research* 2 (1974): 341-343; Fred M. Gotheil, "An Economic Assessment of the Military Burden in the Middle East," *Journal of Conflict Resolution* 18 (September 1974): 502-514; Nadav Safran, *From War to War* (New York: Pegasus, 1969); Mary Kaldor, "The Military in Third World Development," in Richard Jolly, ed., *Disarmament and World Development* (New York: Pergamon Press, 1978).

9. Nicole Ball reviewed the published dialogue regarding each of these potential benefits in "Burdens of Militarization," *International Social Science Journal* 35, 1 (1983): 81-97; for the discussion of military training and attitudes toward modernization, see Lucien W. Pye, "Armies in the Process of Political Modernization," in John J. Johnson, ed. *The Role of the Military in Underdeveloped Countries* (Princeton: Princeton University Press, 1962), and Jong-Chun Baek, "The Role of the Republic of Korea Armed Forces in National Development: Past and Future," *Journal of East Asian Affairs* 3, 2 (Fall/Winter 1983): 292-323.

10. Nicole Ball, "Military Expenditure and Socio-economic Development," *International Social Science Journal* 35, 1 (1983): 81-97; Ron Huisken, "Armaments and Development," in Helena Tuomi and Raimo Vayrynen, eds., *Militarization and Arms Production* (London: Croom Helm, 1983), pp. 3-25; David K. Whynes, *The Economics of Third World Military Expenditures* (Austin: University of Texas Press, 1979); Gavin Kennedy, *The Military in the Third World* (London: Duckworth, 1974); Jose Encinas del Pando, "Economic, Military and Socio-Political Variables in Peru, 1950-1980," *Ibero-Americana* 12, 1-2 (1983); Carlos Portales and Augusto Varas, "The Role of Military Expenditure in the Development Process: Chile 1952-1973 and 1973-1980—Two Contrasting Cases," *Ibero-Americana* 12, 1-2 (1983); Mario Esteban Carranza, "The Role of Military Expenditure in the Development Process: The Argentina Case 1946-1980," *Ibero-Americana* 12, 1-2 (1983); J. Bayo Adekanye, *The Role of Military Expenditure in Nigerian Development,* University of Ibadan, mimeo, 1982.

11. In addition to the works cited in the previous note, see M. Naur, "Industrialization and the Transfer of Civil and Military Technology to the Arab Countries," *Current Research on Peace and Violence* 3, 3-4 (1980): 153-176.

12. Huisken, in "Armaments and Development," p. 20, writes of the "dictatorial impact" that advanced weapons sytems have on technological and industrial development.

13. Harlan W. Jencks, "The Chinese `Military-Industrial Complex' and Defense

Modernization," *Asian Survey* 20, 10 (October 1980): 965-989.

14. Stephanie G. Neuman, "Security, Military Expenditures and Socioeconomic Development: Reflections on Iran," *Orbis* 22, 3 (Fall 1978): 569-594.

15. Nicole Ball, "Defense and Development: A Critique of the Benoit Study," *Economic Development and Cultural Change* 31, 3 (April 1983): 507-524, and Ball, "Defense Expenditures and Economic Growth: A Comment," *Armed Forces and Society* 11, 2 (Winter 1985): 291-297; Susan Helper, "Military Spending and Growth in Developing Countries: A Review of Some Econometric Evidence," paper presented at the Conference on Development and Security in the Third World, Fletcher School of Law and Diplomacy, Tufts University, April 12-13, 1984.

16. C.A.O van Nieuwenhuijze, *Social Stratification and the Middle East: An Interpretation* (Leiden: E.J. Brill, 1965).

17. Ervand Abrahamian, "Oriental Despotism: The Case of Qajar Iran," *International Journal of Middle East Studies* 5, 1 (January 1974): 3-31; Shaul Bakhash, "Center-Periphery Relations in Nineteenth Century Iran," *Iranian Studies* 14, 1-2 (Winter-Spring 1981): 41.

18. Shahrough Akhavi, *Religion and Politics in Contemporary Iran: Clergy-State Relations in the Pahlavi Period* (Albany: State University of New York Press, 1980). Akhavi describes the political bureaucratization of the state after 1953. The evolution of state planning is viewed within the context of bureaucratization in Asbjorn Lovbrock, *State Interventionism, Industrial Growth and Planning in Iran*, master's thesis, University of Oslo, 1977.

19. James A. Bill and Carl Leiden, *The Middle East: Politics and Power* (Boston: Allyn & Bacon, 1974).

20. Barry Rubin, *Paved With Good Intentions* (Oxford: Oxford University Press, 1980).

21. Marvin Zonis, *The Political Elite of Iran* (Princeton: Princeton University Press, 1971), p. 68.

22. For example, see Jack C. Miklos, *The Iranian Revolution and Modernization: Way Stations to Anarchy*, National Security Essay Series 83-2 (Washington, D.C.: National Defense University Press, 1983). For more detailed political analyses of the prerevolutionary period, see John Stempel, *Inside the Iranian Revolution* (Bloomington: Indiana University Press, 1982); Ervand Abrahamian, *Iran Between Two Revolutions* (Princeton: Princeton University Press, 1982).

23. The willingness of governments to undertake short-term risks in the interest of long-term economic benefits is often cited as one of the advantages of state-run enterprises. But very little attention has been paid to the disruptive effects of planning in particular political settings or to its military dimensions. Hossein Bashiriyeh, in *The State and Revolution in Iran 1962-1982* (London: Croom Helm; New York: St. Martin's, 1984), does introduce this issue for Iran.

TWO

Iran's Security Environment

Iran is situated within the Middle East "shatterbelt," a region that historically has been of strategic interest to world powers and one that has experienced prolonged periods of instability within and between countries. Thus, Iran's relations with its neighbors have been dominated by conflict—over relations with world powers, competing political and religious ideologies, ethnic nationalism, unresolved boundary issues, oil policy, and the Arab-Israeli conflict. Adding to the instability, it is a region in which the interested countries have very unequal power.

Iran's rulers have given expression to the hostility of this environment in characterizing the country as surrounded by threats from "all points of the compass" (*tous azimuths*).[1] On several occasions, their fears have been realized. Iranian territory has been invaded and occupied by Soviet and British forces on several occasions from the mid-nineteenth century on through the Second World War. Many Iranians believe that this sort of thing could happen again if the United States and the Soviet Union move closer to a military confrontation in the Gulf.

Threats to Iranian security are seen as political as well as territorial. Thus there is a pervasive anxiety about external meddling in domestic affairs, as well as concerns about the strategic implications of political instability in neighboring states and about ethnic and ideological conflicts that cross national boundaries. Indeed, armed conflicts have often erupted. Within Mohammad Reza Shah Pahlavi's lifetime, Iranian government troops fired on Iraqi forces, on Iranian Qashqa'i, Baluchi, and Kurdish tribal forces, Dhofari rebels in Oman, and *mujaheddin* (Islamic

13

freedom fighters) in Gilan. Until the war with Iraq began in 1980, Iranian
soldiers had fought more within the country than outside it.

This chapter discusses the sources of Iran's insecurity and the
ways the Shah and others have responded to those threats.[2] Historically,
many of the security policies adopted by Iran's rulers have involved
relationships with outside powers. This has occurred because, in addition to the domestic political situation described in the introduction, there
have been so many conflicts within the region that no regime could respond adequately to them all. In actuality, Iran's own military capabilities have never been sufficient to guarantee its security, despite its tre-
mendous oil and gas resources.

FOUNDATIONS OF THE U.S. ALLIANCE

Regardless of the criticisms and the disagreements that occurred over the
years, the Shah's relationship with the United States had a major impact
on the military policies that he adopted and, therefore, on military spending. The Iran-U.S. alliance began to develop during the Second World
War and evolved considerably in the years that followed. American involvement in Iranian military affairs began in 1941, when, on his father's
forced abdication, Mohammad Reza Shah became the titular ruler of Iran.
The military involvement had very political roots. And, throughout his
rule, the Shah continued to equate the security of the monarchy with
Iran's national security.[3]

Over the five years of the Allied occupation of Iran, the Shah was
preoccupied with securing his throne. He had had little political experience, and lacked confidence in his ability to work within the structure of
parliamentary government as it then existed. American diplomats in Teheran felt that Iran needed a strong ruler and recommended that Washington back the pro-American Shah with military support. The Shah was
able to consolidate a domestic base of support in the armed forces, using
the U.S. military assistance as political leverage.[4] Thereafter, he looked
upon the United States and the armed forces as the twin pillars of his regime.

His favorable opinion of the United States was further reinforced
when the Soviet Union refused to withdraw its troops from Azerbaijan,
where a Soviet-backed republican regime had been established in 1945.

The United States applied diplomatic pressure on the Soviet Union, pressing the Shah's case in the United Nations, while the prime minister, Qavam os-Saltaneh, used a combination of parliamentary and diplomatic maneuvering to the same end. Eventually, the Soviet Union withdrew its troops and the Shah was able to personally lead Iranian forces into Azerbaijan and reestablish the central government's authority there.

As far as the Shah was concerned, Soviet intentions toward Iran had been demonstrated by its part in the invasion that sent his father into exile, and its support for Iran's Tudeh (communist) party. In 1950, he signed a Mutual Defense Agreement with the United States that reflected their joint concern over Soviet expansionism. The United States also was a foil for British influence in the country, which had been very pervasive for over a century and which continued in several forms, including the Anglo-Iranian Oil Company's control over Iran's oil resources.

The Shah's intention to expand Iran's armed forces under that agreement was limited by U.S. skepticism over how large a military establishment Iran actually could afford. U.S. Ambassador Wiley reported his view that the Shah's plans would "exceed the financial capacity of Iran."[5] Iran received surplus World War II planes and other military assistance (see below and Chapter 3); however, the relationship continued to be characterized by political rather than military support. This was the situation leading into what has become known as the "Mossadegh crisis" of 1953, when the two-year deadlock between Britain and Iran over oil nationalization developed into a contest for authority between the Shah and Prime Minister Mossadegh. In a now well-documented series of events, the United States helped the Shah's supporters to force Mossadegh's resignation. The oil issue was resolved to the apparent mutual satisfaction of the Shah and the U.S. government by bringing U.S. oil companies into a strong minority position in an international consortium.[6]

Although a certain element of Cold War politics was present in the Mossadegh crisis, the polarization of regional politics along U.S.-Soviet lines developed much more clearly after that time. And the intensity of U.S.-Soviet competition increased the military nature of U.S.-Iranian relations. One of the precipitating events was the 1958 revolution that overthrew the monarchy in Iraq. Following the revolution, Iraq withdrew from the Baghdad Pact (CENTO) and turned to the Soviet Union for military support. The Soviet Union supplied advanced military equipment to Iraq relative to that provided by the U.S. to Iran, and refrained from demanding a formal declaration of alliance from the new Ba'athist government. The MiG-15 had been transferred to Iraq by 1958; by 1962, the first supersonic MiG-19s had arrived in the region.

U.S. military assistance continued to build on its foundation in the Shah's regime with the creation of a domestic counterinsurgency force in 1963, and conventional military assistance increased. At the same time, however, a significant change in the U.S.-Iranian relationship began, reflecting the political turmoil and reactions against foreign alliances throughout the Middle East. In 1961 the United States began to build up its strategic forces in the Indian Ocean, where they were not dependent on the political goodwill of the countries immediately bordering the Soviet Union.

The Shah capitalized on this shift as an opportunity to pursue a policy that he called "positive nationalism," in which he made modest overtures and received equally modest support from the Soviet government. Thus, when the nuclear-armed A-1 and A-2 Polaris submarines moved into the Indian Ocean, the Shah could assure the USSR that Iran "would not grant permission to any foreign country to place rocket bases on Iranian soil."[7] In return, Soviet propaganda attacks on the Shah ended and were replaced by praise for his forceful suppression of reactionary demonstrations against the "White Revolution" reforms (see Introduction). His rapprochement with the Soviet Union helped to discredit Iranian communists, whom he had purged from the armed forces in the mid-1950s.

The cordial relations between Teheran and Moscow, which included a small trade in arms and gas, had no long-term effect on the deepening crisis in the region. In 1969, in the midst of a developing arms race between Iran and Iraq, Britain announced that it planned to withdraw its military forces from all ports east of the Suez Canal, including the Gulf, by 1971. Before the departure date, the Shah met with U.S. Secretary of State Kissinger in Teheran, where it was agreed that Iran would replace Britain as the "policeman of the Gulf."

This resolution was compatible with the immediate interests of both countries. The United States was in the process of extracting lessons from the Vietnam intervention, and the concept of "second-order powers" which could provide military force to support mutual interests in particular regional conflicts had gained currency in Washington. As far as the Shah was concerned, there was sufficient overlap between U.S.-Soviet competition and regional struggles to ensure continuing American support in the form of both its nuclear umbrella and direct military assistance. At home, he was able to portray this alliance as one that was ultimately nationalist in intention and outcome, giving him a political advantage that he had not enjoyed before.

REGIONAL THREATS AND MILITARY RESPONSES

The military relationship between the two countries was based on a more or less mutually-acceptable understanding of their respective security interests, although the compatibility of these interests varied from one arena to another. The area of greatest compatibility was the fear of Soviet expansion. This fear extended into regional (i.e., nonsuperpower) politics and the Shah did not hesitate to point this out. In the early 1970s, the Shah drew attention to a "Soviet-inspired pincer movement" against Iran through Iraq and India. His warning was supported by the announcements of a Soviet-Indian treaty of friendship and cooperation in 1971 and a similar accord with Iraq the following year.

In response to these moves, Iran opposed the Indian policy of keeping the superpowers out of the Indian Ocean (which would primarily have affected U.S. naval forces because the Soviet Union had few ships in the area). The Iranian government also was one of the few in the region to support the construction of an American military base on the island of Diego Garcia, a move to which the Indian government strongly objected.[8]

Within the immediate region, the Shah saw Iran's security and that of his regime as dependent on the fulfillment of four conditions: Iraq's respect for Iran's political and territorial integrity and cosovereignty over the Shatt al-Arab; the political stability of the monarchies on the Arabian Peninsula; the territorial integrity and political stability of Pakistan and, to a lesser extent, Afghanistan; and a secure maritime regime from the Shatt al-Arab in the northern Gulf to the Strait of Hormuz and beyond. He sought to promote these conditions through a combination of military, diplomatic, and economic strategies, policies that were collectively referred to as a regional "pax Iran."

The question of Pakistan presented the most serious overt challenge to the U.S.-Iran relationship. The Shah was very much aware of the constraints on the United States in fulfilling its CENTO guarantees where India was involved. When President Johnson withdrew U.S. military support from Pakistan during the 1965 war with India, the Shah began to talk about CENTO being just a "club" and offered Pakistan sixty F-86 fighters and overflight rights.[9] Following what he bitterly called the U.S.-sanctioned "dismemberment" of Pakistan in 1971, the Shah announced that he planned to acquire weapons that could deter any challenges from regional powers, referring primarily to India.

In 1973, Iran again came to the assistance of the Pakistani government. Pakistan's armed forces were engaged in skirmishes with separatist forces in two regions: the Northwest Frontier Province and Baluchistan. Baluchistan also covers a large area in Iran. The Baluchi separatist movement was more organized in Pakistan than in Iran, but the Shah nonetheless was eager to discourage it from gaining ground anywhere. One of the worst possibilities, as far as the Shah was concerned, was that a weak Baluchistan would be dominated by the Soviet Union. Bordering the Arabian Sea, in the northern reaches of the Indian Ocean, Baluchi forces would be well positioned to interfere with shipping and could pose a direct threat to nearby Iranian naval bases. It was in consideration of these possibilities that the Shah decided to send military supplies and helicopters to the government of Pakistan and to construct a naval base in southeastern Chahbahar.

To the West, Iranian military security involved the Gulf and Iraq, with which it shares a more than one-thousand-kilometer border. Virtually all of Iran's oil is shipped through the Gulf and its southwestern provinces lie along what were virtually unprotected shores. For centuries there has been traffic of goods and people across the Gulf, and Iran has had a more or less direct presence in the Gulf states over those years. Because the United States was committed to protecting the flow of oil to its allies, it was in the Gulf that U.S.-Iranian interests appeared to overlap the most.

The most visible demonstration of the Shah's intent to police the Gulf was his use of the armed forces to occupy three islands on the Arabian side with the close of 1971 and the formal withdrawal of British forces. Before Iran's occupation, sovereignty over the islands, Abu Musa and the Greater and Lesser Tumbs, was claimed by the Arab emirates of

Sharjah and Ras el-Khaymah, respectively. In the face of strong protests from Arab governments,[10] the Shah publicly justified Iran's occupation on the basis of its historic influence in the Gulf and its present-day military capabilities, which overshadowed those of the other conservative Gulf states. At the time, the (Arab) Gulf Cooperation Council had not yet been formed nor did the governments on the Arabian Peninsula attempt to mount any military response.

The second action taken under Iran's new policing role was the deployment of Iranian forces in Oman from 1973 on to help the government end an insurgency in the western province of Dhofar. The insurgents were receiving military assistance from the Soviet Union and had, earlier, from China through South Yemen (the PDRY). The Shah saw Oman as strategically important for two reasons. First, the insurgency was one of several that had threatened to overthrow the monarchies on the peninsula and that had been supported by Egypt and Iraq at various times during the 1960s. Second, Oman lies immediately to the south of the Strait of Hormuz, on the line of shipping toward the Red Sea.

In addition, the intervention provided Iranian counterinsurgency troops with an opportunity to gain experience in using their new weapons and tactical skills. Although it did not develop into a full-blown conflict, the Shah was displeased at the speed with which the United States had extended diplomatic recognition to South Yemen when its leftist government proclaimed the country's independence in 1971. As with Pakistan, these experiences gave the Shah reason to think that the Iranian military's own capabilities would be the best assurance of achieving his security goals in regional conflicts.

During the same time period, Iran was giving military support from its side of the border to Kurdish national resistance fighters in Iraq. Politically significant numbers of Kurds live in Iran, Iraq, Turkey, and the Soviet Union. The governments of all four countries have, on occasion, used the Kurdish national movement to pressure the governments of neighboring countries. The Soviet government assisted in the establishment of a "Kurdish republic" centered in Mahabad, Iran, during the World War II occupation. Throughout the 1960s, relations between the Iraqi government and the Kurds alternated between a tenuous, cautiously negotiated coexistence and armed conflict.

This time, their conflict coincided with the 1973 Arab-Israeli war. The United States and Israel actively encouraged the Shah to intervene in support of the Kurds, forcing the Iraqis to pull some of their military forces away from the Arab-Israeli front. Iran's military support was very direct. Its pilots flew strafing runs into Iraq and Iranian guns "prepared the ground" for resistance fighters to attack Iraqi government troop concentrations. Indeed, Iran and Iraq came very close to outright war.

The question of Iranian-U.S.-Israeli relations warrants separate mention. In addition to containing Soviet military forces and securing oil shipping, Iran and the United States also had a common interest in counteracting the influence of radical Arab states, including Iraq. This shared interest accounts for the development of close military and economic ties between Iran and Israel, to the point that Israel continued to sell weapons and spare parts to Iran after the 1979 revolution. Under the Shah, Iran's de facto alliance with Israel included military and police training for Iran, military supply links, oil for Israel, and Israeli technical assistance in agricultural and other development projects.

At the time, Islamic clergy in Iran decried the government's ties to Israel. The Shah attempted to assume a stance above criticism by being ready to give military assistance to Arab states as well. In addition to Oman, he received an opportunity in the 1973 war by helping to transport Saudi troops to the Syrian front.[11] The policy did not spring from duplicity or a desire to dissimulate on the Shah's part, but from the fact that the Israeli situation raises contradictory opportunities and problems for every Iranian regime. Historically, Iran has repeatedly been involved in conflict with the Arab states; support for Israel offers leverage in those situations.

The Islamic regime's willingness to buy military supplies from Israel is simply one more example of that phenomenon, with the Islamic leaders explaining their decision on the principle that the security of the Muslim community (represented by the Iranian Islamic Republic) comes above all other considerations. Although the Shah did not articulate his security objectives in terms of the Muslim community, he did make an effort to build close and correct relations with the governments of other Islamic countries and was active in the multinational, conservative Islamic Conference.

During the 1970s, the Shah expanded his vision of Iran's security perimeter along with its potential military power. In the Shah's words, Iran's security perimeter was not a matter of "just a few kilometers."[12] He spoke then of Iran achieving "fifth-power status" within a few years, negotiating port facilities as far away as Mauritius and supplying arms to Somalia to protect it against the Marxist government of Ethiopia.[13] He engaged Iran in similar arrangements elsewhere on the African continent.

Iran had a more active military involvement outside its borders during the 1970s than it had had since its forces had fought the Moghul states in India in the eighteenth century at the end of a long period of Persian influence there, after which Persian communities were left scattered across the northern subcontinent. Iranian troops were serving in the Golan Heights with the U.N. forces there, while simultaneously the Islamic Republic's future revolutionary guards (*pasdaran*) were being trained in Lebanon. In the aftermath of the revolution all these forces stayed in place for some time, to the point that the government troops were having resupply problems.

The unusual military activity was accompanied by several important diplomatic initiatives that the Shah launched. After the 1971 war, he began an extended dialogue with Indian Prime Minister Indira Gandhi. Their meetings produced several economic-cooperation and trade agreements, including an exchange of Iranian oil for Indian iron ore destined for Iran's steel mills. In an effort to bring their relations back to a less contentious footing, the two leaders reiterated their formal opposition to outside intervention in regional affairs.

The Shah also had been concerned about Soviet activities in Afghanistan and the opportunity that it might have to gain a permanent foothold there. For a year after Mohammad Daoud had overthrown the Afghan monarch in 1973, he refused to recognize the new government. But, in 1974, he reversed his decision and used the new situation as an opportunity to settle a long-standing dispute between the two countries over the use of the Helmand River.

During this same period, the Shah also was successful in easing the tension with Iraq. In March 1975 he and Iraqi President Saddam Hussein signed an accord, mediated by Algerian President Boumedienne, that brought an end to Iran's military support for the Kurds and acknowledged Iran's cosovereignty over the Shatt al-Arab. In addition, President Hussein agreed to curtail the activities of Iranian opposition groups operating in Iraq, a move that earned him Khomeini's lasting enmity and more than seven years of war.

The role that the Shah's diplomacy played in the tenuous stability of regional politics in the 1970s has received little publicity in comparison to the arms buildup that he participated in. Only one account has been published of a proposal that the Shah made at a 1975 summit meeting of Islamic leaders to conclude a regional arms control agreement.[14] The proposal was in Iran's interest, both because Iran was well armed in comparison to the Arab states and because it would have curbed an increasingly costly arms race. However, according to Robert Hunter, the United States neither supported the proposal nor fully exploited the contribution that Iran's diplomacy was making to U.S. interests in the Gulf.

MILITARY DOCTRINE AND WEAPONS PROCUREMENT

These diplomatic initiatives coincided with the Shah's military initiatives at a time when the Shah had more confidence in Iran's military capabilities than at any time earlier. The security threats that he had identified and that are described above had provided a basis for force deployment and arms acquisition which contributed to that confidence.

Most of the weapons acquisition decisions that the Shah made can be understood in the light of Iran's ultimate reliance on U.S. military power in the region. He could not expect Iran's military forces to be capable of deterring a Soviet invasion by themselves and, therefore, acknowledged Iran's dependence on U.S. military support. Iran's air power could only serve as a "tripwire" against direct attack from the Soviet Union until the United States could mount a military response. Thus, the more Iran could contribute to U.S. military strength in the region, the more secure it would be. For example, AWACS planes that the Shah requested were at least as important to U.S. military capabilities as they were to Iran's. As a result, the U.S. Defense and State departments had tried on two successive occasions to get congressional approval of the sales, but at that time there was too much political opposition to the Shah's arms purchases.*

Against the threat from Iraq, the Shah had adopted a doctrine of "mutual value deterrence" whereby any Iraqi attack would provoke equally damaging retaliation from Iran. In the 1960s, this doctrine and the Soviet "tripwire" doctrine were primarily applied to the air force. In 1962, the United States agreed to supply Iran with F-5 aircraft in response to Iraq's acquisition of Soviet MiGs. In the years that followed, the Shah continued to buy advanced military aircraft as they became available, en-

---

*It is not widely understood in the United States that Iran is not an Arab state and, indeed, has historical conflicts with several Arab states.

larged the maintenance and repair facilities that were used by the air force, and paid for the training of Iranian pilots and technicians.

At the time of the revolution, the strength of the air force was approximately five hundred planes, including the F-14, which was superior to Iraq's Soviet MiG-25 and which could discourage reconnaissance flights over Iran. Boeing 707/747 tankers were acquired, which extended the range of Iran's F-4s to the entire northwest sector of the Indian Ocean.[15] In 1976, the Shah unsuccessfully requested U.S. Airborne Warning and Control Systems (AWACS) planes to improve the response time and fighting efficiency of the air force. He also purchased ground defense weapons, primarily U.S. Hawk and I-Hawk systems (which the Iranian troops could not yet manage without assistance in 1979).

In the mid-1960s, Iran's ground forces were shifted from their concentration on the northern border with the Soviet Union to the Iraqi border. Other aspects of military policy, in addition to the strengthened air force, reflected the central focus on Iraq as it was developing then. One of the largest arms acquisition decisions that were presumably related to defending Iran against Iraqi invasion were the two orders that the Shah placed for Chieftain battle tanks, equipped with laser range finders, raising the total number to 1,960. The size of Iran's tank force would eventually have been equal to those of Israel and Egypt combined.[16]

Iran's long-ignored naval forces also began a period of rapid growth during the 1970s. The navy's role was to protect shipping in the Gulf by maintaining what naval Commander Shahandeh called a "Gulf-wide quick-reaction capability" with the help of air support from new bases along the coast at Jask, Bushehr, and Bandar Abbas (now Bandar Lengeh).[17] Another motivation for strengthening the navy was the India-Pakistan conflict. In seeking congressional support for U.S. arms sales, U.S. administration spokesmen pointed out that the Shah saw a "close relationship between India and the Soviet Union."[18]

India's navy was the second largest in Asia, its ships outnumbering those of Pakistan and Iran (Table 2.1). During the 1971 Bangladesh war, Indian ships operated in the approaches to the Gulf, an action that was not taken lightly by the Shah. Later, Indian ships undertook show-of-flag visits to Um-Qasr, Iraq, lending credence to the notion of the pincer movement that the Shah had described earlier.

As a result of these events, the Shah spoke of developing a "blue water" navy, which meant beyond the Gulf. Iran's main naval facili-

TABLE 2.1

Comparative Military Data:
Iran, Iraq, Pakistan, India, 1976 (and 1971)

	Iran	Iraq	Pakistan	India
Total personnel	300,000 (181,000)	158,000 (95,000)	428,000 (392,000)	1,055,000 (980,000)
Tanks	2,900 (900)	1,390 (905)	1,050 (870)	2,030 (1,450)
Ships (frigates +)	13 (2)	11 (patrol)	10 (12)	54 (28)
Combat aircraft	317 (140)	299 (220)	217 (285)	950 (625)
Military expenditure	$9.5B	$1.2B	$.8B ($.71B)	$2.8B ($1.7B)

Source: International Institute for Strategic Studies (London), *The Military Balance 1976-77* and *1971-72.*

ties at Khorramshahr were enlarged and the naval base at Chahbahar was funded at a high level, with its construction moved forward rapidly. Iranian ships participated in exercises with U.S. naval forces in the area and they began to regularly patrol the entrance to the Gulf, to the west along the Arabian Peninsula, and south to Mauritius. Four Spruance-class destroyers were ordered from the United States, as well as an aircraft carrier. Again, congressional support for the concept of Iran as a regional power was lacking and the request to purchase an aircraft carrier was turned down.

There were also less conventional military threats. The Shah anticipated the possibility that shipping would be disrupted by revolutionary groups on either side of the Gulf, as they had done in 1971 when an oil tanker was attacked near Perim Island in the Red Sea.[19] The "Gulf-wide quick reaction capability" required a counterinsurgency force and a navy that was able to transport ground forces to the Arabian coast. To this end, the navy acquired the world's largest hovercraft fleet and an air-borne brigade was attached to the ground forces. For the counterinsurgency effort in Oman, Iran brought in F-5s, Aq-Bell 205 helicopters, radars, and anti-aircraft guns—all of which were useful in conventional wars as well.

Unconventional threats also included the possibility of armed opposition to the monarchy within the country. Several different counterinsurgency forces were available: the Special Forces, the Imperial Guard, an operational Joint Committee for Fighting Terrorists, and the Gendarmerie. The Gendarmerie was used in actions against gun smugglers and *mujaheddin* operating in the countryside, primarily along a route from Baluchistan in the south through Khorassan to the Caspian region. On the whole, however, the Gendarmerie was poorly armed, provided with only a few outdated planes, and was not an integral part of the counterinsurgency forces. The Imperial Guard was equipped with tanks, antitank weapons, and surface-to-air missiles to defend the Shah in the event of an uprising in the military.

On the whole, however, arming these groups was not very costly relative to the conventional military. And many of the means used to avert a military coup did not involve weapons at all. Officers' promotions were approved by the Shah himself. Officers were rotated between posts regularly and were forbidden to communicate laterally.[20] Limitations were placed on the number of kilometers that armored battalions were allowed to travel within one year.

One further and important question regarding weapons acquisition, connected with Iran's potential "fifth-power status," was (and is) that of the country's nuclear capability. While the Shah ruled, he talked about the nuclear question as a regional issue. Iran signed the Non-Proliferation Treaty and introduced a resolution in the U.N. General Assembly calling for the establishment of a nuclear-free zone in the Middle East.[21] However, after India exploded a nuclear device in 1974, the Shah said that he would reconsider his pledge not to build nuclear weapons "if every upstart in the region gets them."[22]

With the avowed objective of producing nuclear energy in Iran, reactors were purchased from Framatone (France), Kraftwerke Gesellschaft (Federal Republic of Germany), and the U.S. Atomic Energy Commission. A preliminary agreement was reached between Iran and South Africa to exchange South African uranium in return for Iranian financing for an enrichment plant. Work is still proceeding, with foreign technical assistance, on several of the nuclear reactors that were purchased under the monarchy. Presumably, the Shah's policy of keeping Iran's options open has not changed under the Islamic Republic.

POLITICS AND SECURITY

Were the Shah's military preparations necessary and appropriate to the environment within which Iran was situated? One scholar who observed Iranian foreign policy at close range wrote that the Shah could have achieved the same level of security at a lower price *if* the positive results of his "quiet diplomacy" had been factored into arms acquisition decisions and *if* security threats had been identified in more detail so that more specific decisions could have been made about what weapons to buy.[23]

Two of the possibilities for which the Shah prepared were realized: his fall from power and a military invasion by Iraq. However, each event had political origins and the availability of a well-armed military did not provide sufficient insurance to avert either. The Iraqi invasion occurred after months of apparent provocation by Islamic revolutionaries in Iran who wanted to topple the Ba'athist government in Baghdad, particularly President Hussein. President Hussein's advisers judged, incorrectly, the situation in Iran to be sufficiently unstable that the Iranian armed forces would not respond effectively to an attack. That, too, was basically a political judgment, although it included the knowledge that some of the weapons that had been purchased just before the revolution were of little use without continued U.S. assistance.[24]

Other questions were raised, both in the United States and Iran, as to the appropriateness of the weapons purchased. Could Iran's acquisitions have been scaled down without jeopardizing its security? The Chieftain battle tanks, for example, were of questionable defensive value along Iran's largely mountainous border with Iraq.[25] But, with much ground preparation, tanks were used in the war. The Bell Cobra gunships that the Shah purchased also were used in the war and in tribal insurgencies in the wake of the revolution. Islamic government leaders announced that, while they were not interested in much that the industrialized West had to offer, the gunships were an exception in the defense of Islam.

Another issue related to arms procurement is whether the Shah's attempt to protect his regime against potential insurgencies within and outside Iran could have been more successful if it had been more political and less weapons oriented. One of the Shah's close military advisers reflected to this author that the regime overestimated the communist threat and failed to see how much popular strength the mosques were gaining, which indicates that they were concentrating on more conventional threats for which military responses might have been appropriate.

In the event of the revolution, the Shah proved reluctant to use violence and was further discouraged from doing so by various individual U.S. and Iranian advisers. The idea that a military response would cost the Shah support became irrelevant as the revolution quickly proceeded to a conclusion. It seemed to be an accurate reading of political sentiments when it was expressed. After the army did open fire on demonstrators in Teheran in September 1978, one of the Shah's own appointees to the Senate voiced a widely held opinion when he said: "Those whose breasts were pierced and whose brains smashed were Iranian and Muslim. . . . Nowhere in the regulations does it say that soldiers are allowed to shoot and kill."[26]

Whether the military would have continued to support the Shah had they been asked to take arms against those demonstrating against him was a major topic for speculation at the time. A few observers noted that the restrictions the Shah had placed on the officers for the sake of preventing collaboration against him also prevented cooperation on his behalf.[27]

The Islamic regime's armed forces provide a striking contrast to the Shah's in several respects. The regular ground forces have occupied a subsidiary position. In 1979 the ranks of the ground forces were reduced by half, purged of troops believed to be loyal to the Shah. The late defense minister, Mostafa Chamran, spoke of his intention to make politics part of the Islamic regime's security policy. He hoped to build an army with "Israeli efficiency and Cromwell's righteousness."[28]

Shortly after taking power, the new government formalized the creation of a paramilitary force called the *pasdaran*, or revolutionary guards, composed of about forty thousand men and women. At first, they took up the political middle ground between internal security and external defense. According to Abbas Zamani, who commanded the *pasdaran* after the revolution, their duties were: to secure the revolution; to maintain internal and border security; and to promote Islamic culture and ideology.[29] The model for the *pasdaran* was the same as that used by Shi'ite resistance groups in Lebanon, where many of the *pasdaran* were trained.

It was on political grounds that the Shah's security policies were weakest. He did not foster a paramilitary organization comparable to the *pasdaran*, with their ideological conviction, political influence, and military orientation. Instead, mirroring his own Western military training and the predilections of Iran's military advisers, he tended to emphasize technical efficiency and formal training over political zeal, particularly after the arms buildup began.* Soldiers were required to repeat an oath "Shah, God, and country," but their political indoctrination did not extend much further.

SUMMARY

Emile Benoit's study of military spending in developing countries concluded that the "defense burdens" that the governments he studied were willing to carry depended more on the threats they faced than on the amount of resources they could command.[30] In certain respects, this was true of Iran. Arms acquisitions during the 1960s and 1970s were intended to provide security in an environment in which military threats appeared to come from all directions.

The polarization of the region along Cold War lines was both a problem and an opportunity. The Shah saw Iran's security vis-à-vis a direct Soviet military threat as being dependent on the United States and its nuclear umbrella. However, when Iraq and India signed friendship treaties with the Soviet Union and the Soviet government offered and supplied assistance to insurgent groups in Pakistan and on the Arabian Peninsula, the U.S.-Soviet competition demanded, in his view, a stronger and more independent military posture for Iran. For a brief period, this perspective coincided with the United States' policy of working with "second-order powers" to avoid direct involvement in regional conflicts.

Despite their shared interest in containing Soviet military power, the Shah did not trust the United States to defend Iran's interests on the regional level. He also had good domestic political reasons to downplay the alliance. Because of these uncertainties, he purchased a range of

---

*One former adviser described the Shah's enthusiasm for U.S.-style military professionalism as disheartening to long-time and loyal officers, whose traditional skills were not appreciated. The officers were regularly forced to do written examinations on concepts that they were not accustomed to verbalizing, and they faced dismissal for failure.

weapons and support systems that he expected would both meet regional contingencies (eventually without U.S. assistance) and support U.S. military objectives in the meantime. In some cases, the weapons and support systems that Iran acquired met both purposes; in others, weapons were bought that appeared to accomplish neither objective.

While the Shah was acquiring sophisticated weapons and providing military assistance to Iran's neighbors, he also sought diplomatic solutions to several situations of conflict. The one area in which the "pax Iran," with its military and diplomatic aspects, fell short was in responding to the political challenge of Islamic nationalism. The intractable contradiction for all regimes has been the desire for allies and the political anathema of "entangling alliances."

It is a contradiction that is widespread in the Middle East and is responsible, in part, for the dramatic increases in military spending in governments' attempts to become more self-sufficient in an unstable environment. Political stability is the ultimate litmus test for the success of military policies. The appropriate response to internal conflict can set constraints on military responses to external threats. This represents a challenge for Saudi leaders and for the Egyptian government as it did for the Shah before.[31]

NOTES

1. Shahram Chubin, "Iran's Foreign Policy 1960-1976: An Overview," in Hossein Amirsadeghi, ed., *Twentieth Century Iran* (New York: Holmes and Meier, 1977), p. 215.

2. This chapter is not intended to be a comprehensive review of Iranian security policy. Several useful works on that topic include: Shahram Chubin and Sepehr Zabih, *The Foreign Relations of Iran* (Berkeley: University of California Press, 1974); Rouhollah K. Ramazani, *Iran's Foreign Policy, 1941-1973* (Charlottesville: University Press of Virginia, 1975); Alvin J. Cottrell, "Iran's Armed Forces Under the Pahlavi Dynasty," in George Lenczowski, ed., *Iran Under the Pahlavis* (Stanford, Calif.: Hoover Institution Press, 1978), 389-432.

3. See Thomas L. McNaugher, "Arms and Allies on the Arabian Peninsula," *Orbis* 28, 3 (Fall 1984): 489-526, for a discussion of the relationship between internal politics and military security policy.

4. Habib Ladjevardi, "The Origins of U.S. Support for an Autocratic Iran," *International Journal of Middle East Studies* 15 (1983): 227.

5. Barry Rubin, *Paved With Good Intentions* (Oxford: Oxford University Press, 1980), p. 261.

6. The consortium created included six American oil companies (one a consortium itself) which together held forty percent of the shares.

7. Cottrell, "Iran's Armed Forces," p. 400.

8. Diego Garcia is approximately two thousand miles south of Iran. The United

States leased the island from Britain to be developed as a naval and air base.

    9. Shahram Chubin, "The International Politics of the Persian Gulf," *British Journal of International Studies* 2, 3 (October 1976): 204.

    10. William E. Griffith, "Iran's Foreign Policy in the Pahlavi Era," in Lenczowski, *Iran Under the Pahlavis*, p. 378.

    11. Amir Taheri, "Politics of Iran in the Persian Gulf Region," in Abbas Amirie, ed., *The Persian Gulf and the Indian Ocean in International Politics* (Teheran: Institute for International Political and Economic Studies, 1975), p. 276.

    12. Anne Hessing Cahn, "Determinants of the Nuclear Option: The Case of Iran," in Onkar Marwah and Ann Schulz, eds., *Nuclear Proliferation and the Near-Nuclear Countries* (Cambridge, Mass.: Ballinger, 1975), p. 197.

    13. Fred Halliday in *The Middle East*, February 1978, p. 23.

    14. Robert Hunter, "Arms Control in the Persian Gulf," in Andrew J. Pierre, ed., *Arms Transfers and American Foreign Policy* (New York: New York University Press, 1979).

    15. Cottrell, "Iran's Armed Forces," p. 421.

    16. Ibid., p. 413.

    17. *Newsweek*, May 21, 1973.

    18. U.S. House of Representatives, *The Persian Gulf, 1975: The Continuing Debate on Arms Sales*, Hearings before a Special Subcommittee on Investigations (Washington, D.C.: U.S. Government Printing Office, 1975), p. 197.

    19. Chubin, "Iran's Foreign Policy," p. 207.

    20. Marvin Zonis, *The Political Elite of Iran* (Princeton: Princeton University Press, 1971), p. 112.

    21. Cahn, "Determinants of the Nuclear Option," p. 202.

    22. *Keyhan International* (Teheran), September 20, 1975.

    23. Chubin, "Iran's Foreign Policy," pp. 219-222.

    24. William F. Hickman, "How the Iranian Military Expelled the Iraqis," *Brookings Review* 1, 3 (Spring 1983): 19-23.

    25. Steven L. Canby, "The Iranian Military: Political Symbolism Versus Military Usefulness," in Amirsadeghi, *Twentieth Century Iran*, p. 103.

    26. *Keyhan* (Teheran), September 19, 1978.

    27. See L.D. Dillingham et al., *Iranian Arms Acquisition and the Politics of Cooperative Regionalism*, Research Report 40 (Wright Patterson Air Force Base, Ohio: Air Force Institute of Technology, August 1975), AD-AO16-8391.

    28. *Washington Post*, March 21, 1980.

    29. *Merip Reports 86* (March/April 1980), p. 28, an interview with Abbas Zamani published originally in *As Safir* (Beirut), December 1, 1979.

    30. Emile Benoit, *Defense and Economic Growth in Developing Countries* (Lexington, Mass.: Lexington Books, 1973).

    31. McNaugher, "Arms and Allies," and Rodney Jones and Steven A. Hildreth, *Modern Weapons and Third World Powers*, CSIS Significant Issues Series 6, #4 (Boulder, Col.: Westview Press, 1984).

THREE

Trends in Military Spending

During the 1970s, before the revolution that ended the monarchy, the Iranian government spent more money on U.S. weapons and military support than any other non-European country. Members of the U.S. Congress and others were critical of the arms sales and of the Shah's military aspirations. In the last chapter, we looked at the Shah's military policies from the standpoint of his understanding of Iran's security and that of his regime. In this chapter, we shall look at the past record of military spending in Iran, as well as during the 1960s and 1970s, in order to put that period into historical perspective. Iran's rulers sought military security and spent much of the government's resources trying to achieve it long before Mohammad Reza Shah took the throne and allied his government with the United States.

MILITARY ACCOUNTING

First, however, it is important to see how military expenditures were budgeted. Not only does this help us to gain perspective on the validity of military spending statistics, but it also provides a picture of Iran's military establishment and how it evolved during the Shah's rule. The idea of military efficiency, for example, as it took root was mirrored in the type of budgeting that was being done.

In the early 1900s, however, the government's budgeting was very casual. This was in keeping with its significance to economic life in Iran at the time. Government spending accounted for less than five percent of the country's estimated gross national product. The budget was divided into four categories: the army, civil pensions, the royal house-hold, and local administration.

Over time, government expenditures increased in size and com-plexity. More elaborate accounting systems were then adopted. By 1928, the official budget had single entries of the expenses for fourteen mini-stries and offices, as well as "extraordinary expenditures." These last re-ferred to expenditures incurred on behalf of state-owned enterprises (SOEs). No further details were included.

In the 1950s, special categories were created outside the frame-work of the ministries' accounts for public works, construction, and for-eign service. The 1958-59 budget was still a list of item entries for forty-five ministries and agencies.[1] At one point, development expenditures were budgeted separately from the government's operating costs. This practice was abandoned in the late 1960s, however, under pressure from the ministries in a contest for financial control with the Plan Organization (subsequently Plan and Budget Organization).

The idea that the government's accounts should relate to its pol-icy goals was adopted in the early 1960s. Government expenditures were divided among four program areas: public affairs, economic affairs, so-cial affairs, and national defense. Ministry expenses were divided among these. The change was encouraged by U.S. economic advisers, one of whom later observed that "the only technical assistance programs that caught on in Iran were budgeting and poultry raising."

Ministry of War accounts, the largest share of the national de-fense category, were divided among three categories at first: salaries, capital expenditures, and administration. Then, in 1964-65, a five-category system of reporting was begun: personnel, operations and man-agement, procurement, construction, and special expenses. Table 3.1 shows the Ministry of War budget from 1964 to 1977, using these di-visions.

The much smaller budgets of the Gendarmerie and the National Police (a constabulary force) were combined in "internal security" within the national defense budget. In 1968 they were removed from the de-fense budget entirely and transferred to the Ministry of Interior, although the Ministry of War retained control of the Gendarmerie in time of war.

One of the most important characteristics of the national ac-counts as far as estimating military expenditures is concerned is the fact that all the accounting systems used after World War II made a distinc-

TABLE 3.1

Ministry of War Budget by Function (as percentage of total)

Year	Personnel	Operations and management	Procurement, production, and inspection	Construction	Special activities	Debt repayment
1964	59.5	17.8	7.8	.5	4.4	—
1965	55.4	15.9	8.9	1.2	3.8	4.9
1966	50.8	17.4	16.6	1.4	3.8	—
1967	41.5	10.6	17.5	5.9	13.7	10.9
1968	44.0	21.4	17.4	.4	16.9	—
1969	35.2	17.9	15.0	1.4	16.1	14.4
1970	32.9	13.7	21.6	10.1	21.7	—
1971	29.3	12.6	32.9	2.9	22.2	—
1972			not available			
1973	24.9	18.2	37.1	.6	19.2	—
1974	14.7	8.9	63.8	.7	11.8	—
1975	12.8	7.4	69.7	.8	9.3	—
1976	22.9	9.3	59.0	.7	8.0	—
1977	2.36	6.4	61.3	.009	8.6	—
		later years not available				

Source: Iran, Office of Planning and Budget, *Budget Act for the Entire Country*, various years.

tion between the government budget—the expenditures of the ministries—and the state budget, which included the government budget, the accounts of SOEs, and educational institutions and charities patronized by the Court. The state budget typically was one-third larger than the government budget (see Appendix 1). The SOEs included weapons plants, factories for processing food, public utilities, and agricultural corporations, among other enterprises.

The budget reforms could not overcome the political obstacles to financial planning. First, centralized power was not compatible with planning initiatives at lower levels of the bureaucracy. Competition among the ministries also inhibited planning. Information about finances was closely kept and, in many cases, was not available to officials in other ministries who were involved in implementing the same types of programs. Those in the Plan Organization, for example, who were responsible for regional development, did not have access to figures on other ministries' regional expenditures.

PROBLEMS IN ESTIMATING EXPENDITURES

Information about military expenditures was restricted even more than the civilian ministries' accounts. Under law, the formal review process to which the two were subjected was different. Civilian ministries and enterprises were required to submit their accounts to the High Accounting Office and to the director of the Plan and Budget Organization (PBO) before they were transmitted to parliament for approval. Military expenditures were excluded from this requirement. For a brief period during the 1960s, military spending was discussed informally in consultation with civilian officials. But this ceased when the arms buildup began and Iran was no longer receiving military assistance.

There was an auditing process for military expenditures. However, according to a former PBO director, these audits were *ten* years behind. Looking at the budget figures given for national defense in 1976 and 1977 (Appendix 1), it appears likely that the amount given for 1977 was simply carried over from the previous one, as they are exactly the same. Audits would have been valuable but were difficult to undertake during the 1970s, when government spending levels jumped so precipitously that imports could neither be processed nor accurately documented. A former cabinet member recalls that arms imports frequently were recorded as "barley" or "rice" in customs accounts.

The formal accounting system itself and changes that were made in it added to the uncertainty of estimating military spending. "National defense" did not include all military expenditures. Military housing, for example, was budgeted under "social affairs," along with civilian housing. A "discretionary fund" that could be used for military purposes was maintained in the Prime Minister's Office. In 1969, parliament approved a second discretionary fund for defense support, which was made up of "unanticipated" oil revenues and which did not require parliamentary oversight to be spent. (This fund may have contained as much as $2 billion by 1977.)

Other expenditures that were clearly military could not be readily assigned or determined. On the basis of interviews conducted for this study it appears that, in addition to the procurement account, the "special activities" category in the Ministry of War budget was used for arms purchases. The accounts of the military SOEs presented in the state budget were a more serious problem because their size was such that the lack of information could seriously distort military spending estimates.

The number of military SOEs increased rapidly during the 1970s as the government began to invest in military infrastructure, arms production, and weapons maintenance and repair programs (Table 3.2). These activities probably accounted for a large share of Iran's total military budget. The SOEs included Iran Helicopter Industries, Iran Electronics Industries, and Iran Aircraft Industries. The Organization for Ports and Navigation and the Iran Telecommunications Company also were engaged in military-related activities. And, some portion of the Organization for Atomic Energy could probably be considered military as well.

The Military Industries Organization (MIO) served as an umbrella organization for most of the explicitly military SOEs and legally it was accountable to the Ministry of War. In fact, however, at least part of the MIO's funding was outside the ministry budget, as was that of the subsidiary enterprises. Several military SOEs were governed by inter-ministerial boards. Apparently, this did not imply anything about their financing. The military-related civilian SOE's had no formal connection to the military accounts.

The sources from which the SOEs received their funding were not specified in their published budgets. A few were established with

TABLE 3.2

Expenditures of Six State Enterprises
(selected years) ($U.S. thousands)

Enterprise[a]	1969/70	1973/74	1977/78
MIO	26,658	36,780	105,333
IHI	...	1,071	...
IOAE[b]	---	---	145,273
ITC	---	154,438	333,333
IEI	---	...	21,333
OPN	---	25,878	403,733

Source: Iran, Office of Planning and Budget, *Budget Act for the Entire Country*, various years.
aMilitary Industries Organization (MIO), Iran Helicopter Industries (IHI), Iran Organization for Atomic Energy (IOAE), Iran Telecommunications Corporation (ITC), Iran Electronics Industries (IEI), Organization of Ports and Navigation (OPN).
bThe IOAE, ITC, and OPN have civilian functions as well.
... Indicates the organization was in existence during that year, but was not listed in the state budget.
---Indicates the organization was listed, but no budget figures were given.

TABLE 3.3

Military Expenditures: Comparative Estimates
(from official budget data) (millions of rials)

Year	Ministry of War	National defense	National defense, Gendarmerie, and state enterprises[a]	Previous category plus 10%
1973	134,546	134,926	148,408	163,249
1974	372,154	372,647	406,163	446,779
1975	475,524	475,959	564,091	620,500
1976	556,082	566,777	696,795	766,475
1977	555,895	561,066	760,047	836,051

aThe figures for state military enterprises are very low and are not consistent from one year to the next. Those included at least once are: Iran Organization for Atomic Energy, the Organization for Ports and Navigation, and Iran Electronics Industries.

"seed money" from the PBO. The SOEs' detailed financial accounts were considered to be "internal working documents" and were not published. In most years, the SOEs' income and expenditures were portrayed in the published budget by a maximum of four or five figures.

For all these reasons, the estimates that have been made of Iran's military spending can only be a rough approximation of actual expenditures. The official military budget figures from 1948 to 1977 are listed in Appendix 1. After 1964, the figures refer to the category "national defense." The classification used in estimating makes a difference. Table 3.3 shows figures for: (1) the Ministry of War; (2) national defense; and (3) national defense plus expenditures on the Gendarmerie and military and military-related SOEs for the years 1973 to 1977. The national defense budget consists almost entirely of the ministry's budget, so the two are similar. Adding the Gendarmerie and the SOEs makes a greater difference. In 1977 these estimates were thirty-five percent higher than the ministry budgets.

The last column of Table 3.3 contains the previous estimate plus a ten percent correction for omissions. According to former officials who were close to budget-making decisions, ten percent would be a conservative correction; some suggested that a fifty percent adjustment would be more appropriate.

Figure 3.1 compares military spending estimates for Iran made by several sources. Official Iranian government figures for some years were as much as twenty-five percent lower than the figures given by outside sources. From 1968 to 1973, for example, U.S. government estimates were consistently higher than Iran's, particularly for the years immediately preceding 1973. At the time, it is interesting to note, U.S. military advisers were directly involved in preparing Iran's military budgets and had better access to Iranian accounts than after the military assistance programs were ended. As a result, the earlier estimates may have been more realistic, whereas the subsequent figures were closer to the official budgets.

The discrepancy in these estimates was sufficient to warrant caution in drawing conclusions about trends in military spending.[2] Analysts at the Stockholm International Peace Research Institute (SIPRI) compared five different estimates of Iranian military spending; they found a standard error of 26.1 among the estimates.[3] To compensate for these discrepancies as much as possible, examining trends in military spending over

FIGURE 3.1
Estimates of Iranian Defense Expenditures
(billions of current rials)

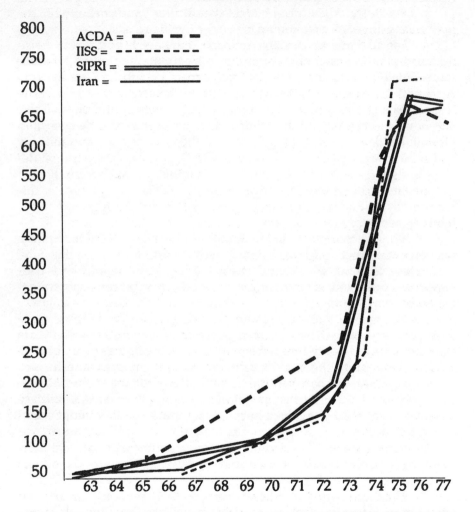

Sources: U.S. Arms Control and Disarmament Agency, *World Military Expenditures and Arms Transfers*; International Institute for Strategic Studies (London), *The Military Balance*; *World Armaments and Disarmament, SIPRI Yearbook*; official government budgets.

a period of time is preferable to looking at military spending and economic growth data on a year-by-year basis.

For this study, official budget data was adjusted to constant Iranian rials using IMF deflators. One of the problems accompanying any kind of international financial comparison is the need to allow for the effects of inflation and foreign exchange rates. Different analysts handle this problem in different ways. The U.S. Arms Control and Disarmament Agency (ACDA) converts rials to constant dollars and constant dollars to current dollars for its estimates. There is no perfect solution; it is simply one more source of distortion that needs to be kept in mind when interpreting the data.

DEVELOPMENT OF MILITARY SPENDING

In the interests of historical perspective, figures on military spending before World War II are included in this section on trends. This affects the way that the data is presented. For many years there was just one comprehensive state budget. Therefore, military expenditures for the entire period are presented as a proportion of the state budget rather than shifting to measures of government spending when those became available. For the purpose of looking at trends, the distinction is not important. This method is desirable as a picture of the extent of military activities in state activities, as distinct from the question of discretionary budget decisions. It does make the level of military expenditures appear to be very low in any particular year because the more common international measures use central government expenditures. Central government expenditures are used below to compare military spending in Iran with other countries.

In Iran, the military accounted for a larger share of state spending in the early part of the twentieth century than it did later (Figure 3.2). In the early 1900s, the military consumed from one-quarter to one-half of the state budget. From 1912 to 1924, it averaged forty percent. The reasons for the sums spent had little to do with external security. Iran was occupied by British troops who were protecting commercial interests in Iran and the approaches to India. Imperial Russian forces occupied some northern sections, storming the parliament building in Teheran on one occasion. But the Iranian military, described as "ragged" and "starving,"[4]

FIGURE 3.2
Military Spending as a Proportion of Iran's State Budget[a]

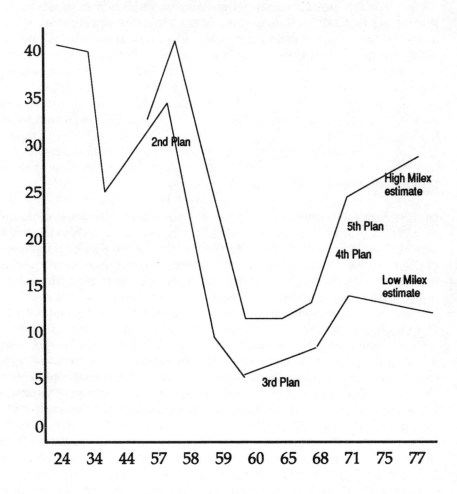

[a]Official Iranian figures for national defense. From 1957 on, the higher estimate takes into account military-related state enterprises, internal security, and arms imports, under the assumption that arms imports often were paid for from funds outside the national defense budget.

was far too weak to force them out. Protests against the foreign presence were staged instead by private citizens and ad hoc guerrilla forces.

For the last of the Qajar shahs, paying military salaries and pensions was more a holding operation than a well-articulated security policy. This was the period of the constitutional revolution, during which Mohammad Ali Shah Qajar struggled with the constitutionalists for control over the government, relying on the comparatively well-organized Cossacks during the first years of the revolution. On several occasions, however, it was not the Shah's troops that were decisive, but tribal and ad hoc contingents. In light of the troops' irrelevance, the explanation for the high levels of military spending must be that the Shah, and even more so his son, Ahmad Shah Qajar, simply kept up the salary and pension obligations that had been assumed in more stable times in the hope that the troops would remain loyal.

The Court had obligations to its extensive household, and the government had begun to make expenditures on schools during the nineteenth century. But, other than that and internal administration, the military was the only demand on the state treasury. Despite the proportion of the budget that was relegated to the military, however, many of the troops were ill-paid and the Shah eventually came to mistrust their loyalty. During that period it was not the level of military spending, per se, that was the political issue but the contest for military loyalty and the fact that the expenditures were underwritten by foreign loans.

Military appropriations continued at a high level for the next decade and then entered a gradual downward trend that lasted until the mid-1950s. Military spending dropped to twenty-seven percent of the state budget in 1936. By 1939 it had declined to fourteen percent, even though overall government spending was increasing. The decline in military spending during the 1930s is particularly interesting because Reza Shah came into power through a coup d'etat as a former Cossack officer and minister of war. While he served as minister, he took control of the Department of Indirect Taxation so that he would be able to pay the troops regularly, a political necessity that he had experienced directly under the Qajars.

After initial fiscal reforms, Reza Shah proceeded to reorganize the military establishment. With the attention given to organization, he put the military on a sounder footing without the expenditure of vast sums of money. The reduction in military spending also was facilitated by the accomplishment of several of the Shah's military objectives, particularly improvements in internal security. Priorities changed. Reza Shah turned his attention and the government's finances to the economy. Like the Turkish modernizer Mustafa Kemal, whom he admired, the Shah believed that the initiative for industrialization would have to come from the state. Funds were provided for building roads and other infrastructure, and no less than 150 state enterprises were established for processing and manufacturing goods and other services.

From that time on the growth of the state continued, although the shift in financing priorities that was evident under Reza Shah was absorbed in rising military spending and never reappeared. The state's role in the economy increased further during the rule of Mohammad Reza Shah. In 1959-60, state spending amounted to twenty-three percent of the GNP; in 1970-71, forty-three percent; and, in 1975-76, *sixty-eight* percent! Military expenditures increased in the same manner as did state spending—from three, to eight, and then to fourteen percent of the GNP over that period of seventeen years.

Within this general trend, military spending fluctuated in response to factors such as the state of the economy and domestic and external political events. Several periods can be identified. As a proportion of the state budget, military expenditures were relatively low from 1949 to 1952, from 1959 to 1964, and from 1975 to 1978. The years during which military spending rose especially rapidly were 1952 to 1954, 1957 to 1958, and 1965 to 1971.

Negotiations with the United States for military assistance influenced the Shah's military policies and spending decisions. Following the Second World War, the Shah was intent on building up Iran's armed forces as rapidly as possible in order to strengthen his throne and to repair the disruption caused by the occupation and his father's abdication. In 1949 the Shah announced plans to put 300,000 men in uniform and to acquire 150 tanks and several hundred aircraft.[5]

However, the U.S. government discouraged these plans, despite the decision to support the Shah. First, the Truman administration was more concerned with containing Soviet expansion in Europe than along the northern rim of Southwest Asia. After Soviet troops were withdrawn from Azerbaijan, Iran slipped into the position of a "strategic backwater."[6] Second, the emphasis in Washington on postwar economic reconstruction was applied to Iran by advising the Shah that he should delay military investments until the economic situation could be improved.

Little aid was forthcoming for this purpose despite the fact that the Allied occupation was a precipitating factor in Iran's economic difficulties. Greece and Turkey received $211 million in U.S. aid; Iran shared $27 million with the Philippines and Korea.

Military expenditures were kept at a relatively low level for a few years. Gifts of weapons and military supplies from the United States made up some of the difference between the Shah's objectives and U.S. preferences, but not all. In later years, the United States was to gradually lose some of its leverage over the Shah's decisions and to become more sympathetic toward his views on military policy.

A precipitate decline in military spending occurred between 1951 and 1952—from $48 million to $23 million, a decline of fifty-four percent in constant 1975 dollars. Prime Minister Mossadegh's nationalization of Iran's oil production and the subsequent British-initiated boycott of Iranian oil proved to be the most effective brake on military spending. The oil boycott drastically reduced government revenues and simultaneously increased domestic opposition to foreign military assistance.[7] Mossadegh saw the army as the Shah's most important ally in their contest for power and encouraged the parliament (Majles) to reduce the army's budget. When Mossadegh was removed from office, the military budget doubled.

From 1955 to 1962, an erratic spending cycle occurred that again appeared to be a response to the politics of military assistance. Military spending fell slightly in 1955, rebounded in 1958, fell considerably in 1959, rose in 1960, and dropped again in 1962. The steep rise in military spending between 1957 and 1958 occurred despite pressure from the Eisenhower administration on the Shah to cut inflation rates and the trade deficit by reducing military spending.[8] The military budget was not cut, but overall government spending was.

In 1959, the governments of the two countries signed a bilateral military agreement and Iran's military budget was reduced. The issue was temporarily resolved and the Shah continued his support for a U.S. alliance despite its unpopularity at home. He had already brought Iran into CENTO at a time when other governments in the Middle East were reluctant to join. And, in the wake of the bilateral agreement, he withstood unusually strong parliamentary pressure to deny extraterritoriality to U.S. military personnel.

The question of how the Shah should rule Iran was raised again by the Kennedy administration, which came into office with the intention of pushing social and economic reform in less industrialized countries as a way to stop the spread of communism. In Iran, the Shah was still reacting to the Mossadegh crisis. Several cities continued to be under martial law. The army's loyalty was crucial and the Shah was reluctant to cut its funds. Communists had been purged from the military; he courted the support of traditional groups, including the clergy, by not taking any positions that would alienate them. He also had made a tentative gesture in the direction of democratic process by allowing two well-controlled political factions (which he called political parties) to operate in parliament.

In seeming disregard of the tenuousness of the Shah's situation and his ability to respond appropriately to it, the Kennedy administration cut off $30 million in military aid, pending the introduction of economic reforms. In 1961 the Shah was urged to appoint as prime minister Dr. Ali Amini, a man who had served in Mossadegh's cabinet and who was understood to share the Kennedy administration's perspectives about social and economic change. After considerable pressure on the Shah, in 1962 a land redistribution program was initiated and a year later the program was incorporated into the "White Revolution," a series of edicts including industrial profit-sharing, the formation of health and development corps, the nationalization of water and grazing land, and so forth. Conflict arose over these reforms on the street while parliament remained closed for more than two years.

At this point the Shah was resisting cuts in military spending, just as he had done during his negotiations with the Eisenhower administration. A historian, Ervand Abrahamian, wrote that Prime Minister Amini did want to see military expenditures reduced along with other measures to carry the economic reform into the political arena.[9] The Shah resented U.S. interference and believed that it would ultimately damage his own political position; he finally removed Prime Minister Amini and Minister of Agriculture Hassan Arsanjani from office. According to Abrahamian, Amini tried and failed to get support from the United States in the conflict over military spending so that he could fend off the Shah's opposition.

In 1965, the rate of growth of military spending began a steady upward trend that continued until 1976 (Figure 3.3). Previously, from 1960 to 1965, the average annual rate of increase was nineteen percent. From 1965 to 1970 the average was forty-four percent annually, and between 1970 and 1975, it remained at forty-one percent. The proportion of

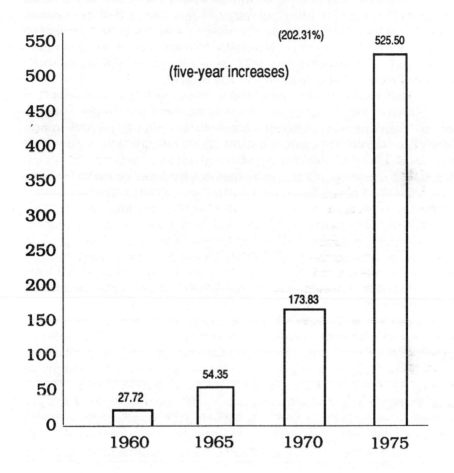

FIGURE 3.3
Trends in Military Spending[a]
(in constant 1975 rials)

[a]Official national defense figures adjusted to take inflation into account from data in U.S. dollars, *Yearbook of National Accounts Statistics, 1979.* Figures in parentheses show the increase in military spending during the intermittent five-year periods.

military spending within total government expenditures was as high as it had been at the beginning of the century.

Increasing military expenditures were accompanied by a major shift in the content of military purchases. Beginning in 1966, the portion of the Ministry of War budget allocated to salaries began to decline (Table 3.1). As weapons imports increased, so did their share of the military budget. Consequently, by 1977 the relative shares of salaries and weapons procurement in the budget were reversed.

Financed by oil revenues, which rose from $2.4 billion in 1972 to $17.4 billion in 1974, most of the weapons that were purchased were imported. Weapons manufacturers went to Iranian officials directly to promote sales, despite objections from American officials who argued that this took away one source of their influence on events in Iran. On the Iranian side, weapons purchases were handled by a few people who were personally loyal to the Shah; the two key people were General Hassan Toufanian, chief of arms procurement, and General Mohammad Khatemi, head of the air force and of the army airborne divisions. Decisions about weapon procurement were seldom discussed outside this group.[10] The process discouraged careful assessments of spending and planned procurement schedules.

By 1975, oil revenues began to level off. The Shah accused the oil consortium of deliberately lowering the amount of oil it was taking from Iranian fields. By 1976, cabinet meetings in Iran produced unusually open and acrimonious debate on what some felt to be excessive military spending. In Washington, congressional opposition to selling advanced weapons to Iran grew and U.S. military officials worried about the chaotic situation that the sudden spurt in imports had produced in Iran's ports, inventories, and support structures. The Carter administration had announced that arms sales would be linked to the recipient government's performance on human rights and urged the Shah to permit more political dissent. In the course of these events, the growth in military expenditures slackened markedly.

Several large weapons contracts were canceled during 1978. When Shahpour Bakhtiar became caretaker prime minister in December, he canceled weapons orders worth as much as $10 billion. By this time the U.S. government was urging Bakhtiar to sign a "memo of understanding" that Iran would honor the arms contracts. After the revolution, arms imports were cut still further. Despite the war with Iraq, the downward trend continued into 1981-82, when parliament was reported to have voted to reduce the military budget. Later, the war's continuation changed the trend once again.

COMPARING MILITARY EXPENDITURES

As was suggested earlier, military expenditures are expected to reflect military security policies. Iranians see their security environment as a hostile one, partly because the Middle East region has experienced so much conflict. Thus it is useful to look at this region as a whole, since in it military spending has been higher than in other areas.

In 1975 it was the highest, with an average of 13.1 percent of total GDP devoted to military activities. At 3.6 percent, East Asia was the second highest outside the U.S. and Soviet alliance systems. Military funds have been spent throughout the region on increasingly sophisticated and expensive weapons, which arms-exporting countries have been willing to sell despite their potentially destabilizing effects.[11] Oil revenues and political leverage over the exporters have provided the funds to maintain spending at this level.

In comparison to other countries in the Middle East, Iranian military spending was not very high during the 1960s, either in absolute terms or in proportion to government spending. Over the next decade, Iran outspent every other government in the Middle East. However, taken as a proportion of government spending and GNP, Iran's military expenditures still were average for the region.

Potential armed conflict with Iraq was a central focus of Iranian military security planning during the last decade of the Shah's rule. The arms race that ensued was more costly for Iraq than for Iran. After 1972, Iran's military expenditures averaged twenty-six percent of total *government* (not state) spending; Iraq's, thirty-seven percent. Revised U.S. Arms Control and Disarmament Agency estimates, published in 1984, put Iraqi military spending at nearly half of the total government budget.[12] The first large increase occurred in 1973, during the October War and the Kurdish rebellion. The second occurred between 1980 and 1981, when it was clear that the war with Iran was going to be a protracted one.

The Iraqi government also spent a larger proportion of its GDP on the military than did Iran (Table 3.4). In terms of other indicators of military effort, however, Iran spent more. In proportion to the size of its

TABLE 3.4

Comparative Levels of Military Spending: Iran, Iraq, Turkey,
Egypt
(constant 1978 $U.S. millions, percentage of GDP)

Year	Iran		Iraq		Turkey		Egypt	
	$	%	$	%	$	%	$	%
1955	291		140		775		489	
1960	577	4.3	313	7.1	892	5.1	513	5.8
1965	862	4.9	563	8.8	1,318	5.0	974	8.0
1970	1,906	6.6	841	11.2	1,448	4.3	2,271	16.2
1975	10,168	13.1	2,049	11.7	2,351	4.6	5,756	33.4
1976	11,031	12.5	2,010	11.2	3,208	5.8	5,004	24.9
1977	8,902	10.8	2,100	10.4	3,320	5.8	5,239	25.1
1978	9,506		1,988		2,557	5.1	3,325	
1979	4,943		1,968				2,840	

Source: World Armaments and Disarmament, SIPRI Yearbook 1980.

population (about three times that of Iraq), its armed forces, and its terri-
tory, Iran's military budget was larger.[13] Arms data also show that the
Iraqi government did not attempt to maintain equivalent air power (see
Table 2.1).

Egypt and Turkey—comparable to Iran in size and population—
had very different military spending records. As a proportion of GNP,
Turkey's was consistently low for the Middle East. There are several explanations for this from the standpoint of Turkey's strategic situation. It
is not directly involved in the Arab-Israeli conflict, although Islamic politics are extremely important within the country. As a member of NATO,
Turkish leaders take the U.S. commitment to its security more seriously

than the Shah did with CENTO. And, Cyprus has been a problem within NATO, but it has not posed a threat to Turkey's strategic interests.

In contrast, the burden of military expenditures that the Egyptian government has been willing to carry has been heavier than Turkey's and Iran's. Since 1974 Egyptian military spending has absorbed an ever larger share of its GNP, despite the peace treaty with Israel. Some considerations are: (1) the loyalty of the military to the government, (2) maintaining a position of leadership in the Arab world, and (3) armed conflict in northeast Africa. In the latter region, Egyptian leaders are concerned about increased Soviet activity, Sudan's internal political stability, and Libya's aggressive pursuit of its interests.

Despite Egypt's pressing economic problems, therefore, the government increased military expenditures to one-third of its GNP in 1975 and maintained them at roughly that level for several years thereafter. At the same time, U.S. military assistance increased as a result of the Camp David Accords and developing strategic military cooperation between the two countries. Half of the U.S. assistance from 1976 to 1986 was in the form of loans, so that true military costs will only become visible later.

SUMMARY

Reliable data on military spending is difficult to acquire for any country. Iran is no exception. The various means by which the government obscured military spending figures are ample evidence of their political significance. In Iran, the Shah's opponents looked at the military as part of the regime, even though that image understated the liveliness of politics within the armed forces. The fact that military spending involved close military ties with the West also politicized the issue.

Iran's military suppliers also had a political interest in the level of military spending. With the exception of the Nixon administration, every U.S. president since World War II pressed the Shah to reduce military spending and to accomplish economic and political reforms if he wished to receive military assistance. The Shah resisted the pressures to reduce spending, but did make most of the reforms requested. And, the most rapid increase in military spending occurred within the context of the U.S. alliance.

In comparison to other periods in Iran's history and other countries in the Middle East, military spending under Mohammad Reza Shah was not exceptionally high. At the turn of the century, a primary function of the state was to financially maintain a military establishment, something that the last Qajars continued to do despite the breakdown of internal order. At that time most of the funds went to salaries and pensions, and they continued to account for the largest share of military spending until the 1960s.

The most significant development in military spending from the standpoint of its economic impact was the shift of expenditures from personnel to weapons, most of which were imported. The chapters to follow bring out the implications of this change for the Iranian economy.

NOTES

1. Iran's calendar year begins in March and therefore spans two Gregorian calendar years.

2. Michael Brzoska, "The Reporting of Military Expenditures," *Journal of Peace Research*, 18, 3 (1981): 261-275.

3. Stockholm International Peace Research Institute, *World Armaments and Disarmament, SIPRI Yearbook 1980* (London: Taylor & Francis, 1980), p. 15. Other sources for the comparisons with official Iranian data were the Arms Control and Disarmament Agency, *World Military Expenditures and Arms Transfers,* and the *United Nations Statistical Yearbook.*

4. Ervand Abrahamian, *Iran Between Two Revolutions* (Princeton: Princeton University Press, 1982), p. 91, quoting E.G. Browne, *A Year Among the Persians.*

5. C.D. Carr, "The United States-Iranian Relationship 1948-1978: A Study in Reverse Influence," in H. Amirsadeghi, ed., *The Security of the Persian Gulf* (London: Croom Helm, 1981), p. 62.

6. Ibid., p. 60.

7. Sepehr Zabih, *The Mossadegh Era: Roots of the Iranian Revolution* (Chicago: Liberator Press, 1981), p. 71.

8. Barry Rubin, *Paved with Good Intentions* (Oxford: Oxford University Press, 1980), p. 102.

9. Abrahamian, *Iran Between Two Revolutions,* p. 422.

10. For example, the commander of the army was not informed until after the fact that British Chieftain tanks had been purchased to replace the M-60s that the army had been using.

11. Robert Litwak, *Security in the Persian Gulf,* Vol. 2, *Sources of Interstate Conflict* (London: International Institute for Strategic Studies, 1981), discusses the question of advanced weapons transfers.

12. U.S. Arms Control and Disarmament Agency, *World Military Expenditures and Arms Transfers 1972-1982* (Washington, D.C.: USACDA, 1984), p. 30. The 1981 data for Iraq contained unexplained discrepancies.

13. Ruth L. Sivard, *World Military and Social Expenditures 1980* (Leesburg, Va.: World Priorities, 1980), p. 26.

FOUR

Arms Production

As many countries take steps to become self-sufficient in weapons production, investments in arms industries are increasing. How these industries affect the economies of the less industrialized countries deserves more attention. The continuing technological revolution in weaponry has increased the costs of arms production. But for many countries the export market for weapons has provided a significant source of foreign exchange. Beyond these surface effects, understanding the impact of arms production on economic growth requires knowing more about the structure of arms industries in less industrialized countries and about the arms production process and its relationship to other sectors in the economy.

Modern weapons production is concentrated in a relatively small number of countries. The United States dominates the industry globally, with more than 1,100 corporations and 700,000 workers engaged in research and the development and production of weapons.[1] Nearly half of all licenses issued for weapons production in 1978 were from U.S. firms. The remainder were held by Britain, France, West Germany, Sweden, and the Soviet Union. This list has grown since then and will continue to do so, as industrial capabilities develop and the arms trade fosters licensed and unlicensed adaptations of weapons originally produced in the countries named. Israel, Brazil, and China, for example, were actively producing for export in the mid-1980s.

Much of the aircraft and missile production that takes place outside the major arms-producing countries is carried out under licensing agreements or as coproduction. Production agreements between countries take one of the following forms: "turnkey" projects, in which nearly all aspects of the production process are imported; assembly from imported parts; indigenous production, in which only the license is obtained from external sources; or codevelopment, in which an original design is produced from collaborative research.[2]

Because arms production in most countries is not a predominantly indigenous process, it can be considered as an extension of arms imports—from the initial agreements to buy arms, parts, and designs, to "back-end" arrangements for the provision of ongoing technical support.[3] The link between domestic arms industries and arms imports accounts for the contrasting perceptions of the military industrialization process that are held by the participants in that process. Within the countries trying to enter the industry, it has been hoped that arms production would contribute to the domestic industrialization process. General Katorijan, head of Iran's armed forces' control bureau under the Shah, described Iran's arms industries as a *precondition* for industrialization.[4]

The perceptions of the supplier countries have been quite different. The director of the British Defense Sales Organization stated that substantial profits were to be earned from military industrialization in the Third World, specifically from building weapons plants and repair shops.[5] U.S. weapons manufacturers described the expansion of the Iranian market for support services as the number of in-country repair, maintenance, and production facilities increased.[6] In the mid-1970s, it was not primarily the weapons themselves that were being imported, but weapons-related material. About half of Iran's military imports consisted of software: training, maintenance, and electronics engineering.[7]

This chapter gives a short history of arms production in Iran and describes the in-country repair, maintenance, and production projects that were initiated during the 1970s. The origins of these projects and the way in which they were organized were different in several respects from the earlier development of arms production in the industrialized countries. The differences make it difficult to draw conclusions from the past about how military industrialization will affect the evolution of civilian industry.

THE HISTORY OF ARMS PRODUCTION

The government of Iran began to produce armaments and military supplies in the 1850s: cannons, light arms, uniforms, and other items.[8] Every regime to hold power since then has concurred with the idea that arms production is vital to Iran's military security. The manufacture of small arms and explosives was developed further in the 1920s and 1930s. The main ammunitions factory established at Parchin (East Teheran) has been operating continuously for more than fifty years.

A third period of focus on arms production occurred in the late 1960s and 1970s. Most of these projects, as we shall see, were built on foreign support of various kinds. Unlike many of these later repair, maintenance, and production projects that relied on foreign technicians, Parchin is run primarily by Iranians and has been kept open by the Islamic government. The distinction made reflects an undercurrent that has been present in arms production decisions since the beginning. Although the importance of military industries has been commonly acknowledged, regimes differed on the question of how imported technology should be integrated into the process.

The government's efforts to make Iran self-sufficient in military equipment have always been hampered somewhat by lack of domestic financing and available technology. During the last decades of the nineteenth century, the Qajars found it easier to turn to foreign military assistance, which the great powers were competing to provide. In attempting to build up Iran's armed forces, the government has brought in military advisers from several countries. In 1885 Iran began to buy German weapons and to employ German military instructors. Russians equipped and led the Iranian Cossack brigade. In southern Iran, the British founded and armed the South Persia Rifles. The Gendarmerie was run by Swiss advisers.

With the collapse of the Qajar dynasty, self-sufficiency became a priority again. Foreign political and military intervention had been rampant. So, in 1919, when Britain offered Iran a comprehensive military treaty, parliament rejected it. When Reza Shah came to power in 1925, he began to diversify Iran's military production. Gunpowder was produced at Parchin; and an iron foundry and brass rolling mill, essential for arms production, were established. Rather than seek help from Britain or the Soviet Union, Reza Shah requested assistance from Germany and Czechoslovakia. In the 1930s, Brno (Mauser) rifles, machine guns, and 105mm long and short Czech anti-aircraft guns were being fabricated in Iran, using steel and machine tools imported from Germany.[9]

Aircraft were assembled in Iran beginning in the 1930s, first with German and then with British assistance. By the time that World War II broke out, Iranian technicians had successfully assembled British Hawker Fury I planes and Hawker Hinds. Progress toward self-sufficiency was slow, however. Iran's dependence on imported spare parts and guns was critical, because Britain objected to the German presence in Iran. When the Allies invaded Iran, a few pilots took off in their unarmed planes as a symbolic gesture of defiance, but the reality was that Iran was defenseless.

The war set back the development of arms production in Iran by at least two decades. After the Allied invasion, German technicians working at Parchin were deported. Soviet troops occupying Teheran took over the factories and produced ammunition for their own use. The aircraft industry was not reinstated until the 1960s.

By that time, Iran was manufacturing many more military products than before: explosives, small arms, rocket propellants, vehicles, batteries, and radios. A Ministry of Economy survey published in 1972 identified seven military industries, which it listed as subsidiaries of the Military Industries Organization (MIO): (1) chemical institutions; (2) ammunition factories; (3) metallurgy factories; (4) radio manufacturing plants; (5) engineering plants; (6) manufacturers of "war means"; and (7) manufacturers of batteries. According to official statistics, 7.6 percent of government investments made under the Fourth National Development Plan (1968-1972) went into these industries.[10]

In the late 1960s, Iran's arms buildup included a number of contracts to cover the repair, maintenance, and production of weapons. The contracts covered most of the advanced weapons that were being imported. The Shah's immediate objective was for Iranians to be able to repair their own weapons during periods of armed conflict. At the time of their purchase, some of the electronically guided weapons had to be returned to the supplier country for repair.

One of the new enterprises was linked to the Shah's concept of Iran as the focal point of a regional security arrangement with Pakistan and Turkey. He suggested on several occasions that the governments of the three countries should combine their arms production programs.[11] When he apparently did not get a positive response from Pakistan and Turkey for a large-scale, combined program, he opened the Iran Electronics Industries (IEI) missile repair facility in Shiraz to Pakistan. Cooperation in repairing and redesigning antitank missiles continued after the revolution.

By 1979, Iran's various production projects were at different stages of completion. Some weapons were being produced under license, using a combination of imported and domestic materials. Imported weapons were being modified with some assistance from foreign technicians; and, a few components for imported weapons were being fabricated in Iran.

Since the revolution, rifles, machine guns, and ammunition are still being produced there. In a few instances, Soviet designs have been substituted for Western products. The Islamic government preferred to deal with neither superpower, however, and in 1987 concluded an agreement with China to import five weapons factories. With the stimulus provided by the war, Iranian technicians repaired and maintained aircraft on their own and took other initiatives such as altering the design of antitank rockets to accommodate the lack of imported launchers.

Maintenance, Repair, and Production Projects

The agreements negotiated from the late 1960s onward included tactical missiles,[12] aircraft, armored vehicles, and communications, electronics, and software projects (see Appendix 2). The projects are described below, with particular emphasis on the extent of indigenous and foreign contributions. The chronology of their initiation can be understood in the context of military security decisions described in Chapters 2 and 3.

Small arms and ordnance. During the last years of the Shah's rule, factories run by the MIO were producing small arms, machine guns, and ammunition at Parchin, Saltanatabad, Esfahan, Shiraz, and Dorud (see Table 4.1). Had the revolution not intervened, a much larger ordnance complex was to have been built in Esfahan. A proposal for the complex was concluded with Millbank Technical Services (U.K.) in 1977-1978. The initial cost of the plant, which was to produce tank ammunition and gun barrels, was estimated at $1,275 million. Wimpey-Laing (U.K.) contracted to build a tank repair facility at the same location. Bofors (Sweden), which already was involved in the manufacture of explosives and rocket propellants in Teheran, expected to expand its operations to Esfahan.

Germany's pre-World War II involvement in military production was reinstated under the Federal Republic of Germany (FRG).[13] An FRG government-owned firm, Fritz-Werner, was under contract with the MIO

TABLE 4.1

Ordnance Produced at MIO Factories, Iran

Product	Origin of technology	Comments
Ammunition		
.30-inch	—	Unconfirmed
7.62-mm	FR Germany	For rifles and MGs
9.-mm	—	For MPs
.45-inch	FR Germany	For pistols
.50-inch	—	For MGs
20.-mm	FR Germany	For AA guns
23.-mm	USSR	Unconfirmed, for Soviet AA guns
35.-mm	Switzerland	Unconfirmed, Oerlikons
105.-mm		Unconfirmed, howitzers
155.-mm		Unconfirmed, howitzers
Mortars		
60.-mm		Mortar and shells
81.-mm		
120.-mm		
160.-mm		
Small arms		
PSSH-41a submachine gun	USSR	Limited production during and after WWII; Iranian design: Model 22 since early 1960s
G-3 rifle	FR Germany Heckler und Koch	
MG1A1	FR Germany Rheinmetall	
Larger-caliber weapons		
35.-mm AA-cannon		Unconfirmed
20.-mm AA-gun		Unconfirmed
RPG-7 rocket	USSR	Reverse engineering in Iran
BM-21		
rocket and launcher	USSR	Unconfirmed, reverse engineering
155.-mm gun barrels	USSR	Reverse engineering, with FRG

Sources: SIPRI and the author.

for the licensed production of MG1 and MG3 guns and munitions, manufactured at Saltanatabad (Teheran). Technicians from several other NATO countries were also engaged in the manufacture of explosives there.

Guided weapon systems. Under the Shah the Iranian armed forces acquired a variety of guided weapons. Table 4.2 lists the maintenance and repair contracts negotiated during that period as part of arms purchase agreements. The one project not contracted in this manner was an in-country reverse engineering project involving Soviet RPG-7 and BM-21 rockets and SAM-7 missiles.

The Iranian government signed five contracts for the maintenance, repair, and assembly of air defense systems and antitank weapons. In 1971 the IEI contracted with Emerson to repair TOW and FGM-77A Dragon systems for Pakistan and Yemen. A contract to maintain the AGM-65A Maverick and BGM-71A TOW systems was signed in 1975 and placed under the management of IEI's missile division. The contract stipulated that IEI would produce subcomponents and assemble two thousand TOW and Maverick missiles.

In 1976, IEI and the British Aircraft Corporation (BAC) entered into an agreement for the development and assembly of 2,500 Rapier half-tracked, low-level anti-aircraft missiles, to be undertaken by the jointly owned Irano-British Dynamics Corporation.[14] The Iranian government agreed to underwrite all the development costs incurred for this project by the British government, in return for which the BAC would train Iranian engineers and technicians. The production of seventy-five missiles per month was supposed to begin in June 1980, probably in Parchin; but the project was canceled in 1978.

The Shah was willing to underwrite manufacturers' development costs on several advanced weapons, such as the Rapier missile. Reportedly, the Shah wanted, in return, invitations for Iranian engineers to participate in the research and development of the weapons. In at least one case, Iran's request to participate in the development of a U.S.-designed missile, permission was denied. The explanation for the refusal offered to this author was that the request was unrealistic, that the Shah did not understand how long it would take for Iran to build up a scientific and technical capacity beyond that necessary for simple base-level maintenance.

TABLE 4.2

Weapons Purchases and Repair Contracts

Manufacturer/ weapon	First purchase order	Contractor for repair and maintenance	Repair/ maintenance contract date
Aircraft			
Bell Model-214ST, Model-209, AH-IJ	1973	Iranian Helicopter Industry (IHI)/Bell (USA)	1976
Northrop F-5A, F-5B, F-5E	1965	Iranian Aircraft Industries (IACI)/Northrop (USA)	1970
Lockheed RT-33, T-33A, C-130E, C-130H, P3F	1956	IACI/Lockheed (USA)	1975
Augusta-Bell 205, 206A1B, 212, CH-47	1969	IHI/Augusta-Meridionali (Italy)	1974
Grumman F-14	1973	Grumman Iran[a]/Grumman (USA)	
Armored vehicles			
M-47/M-48	1958	Military Industries Organization (MIO)/Bowen McLaughlin/York (USA)	1970
Vickers Chieftain, Fox, Scorpion	1971	MIO/Vicker	1971
Missiles			
Hughes Aircraft BGM-71A TOW, AGM-65A Maverick, AIM-54A Phoenix	1971	Iranian Electronic Industries (IEI)/Emerson (USA), Westinghouse (USA), Hughes (USA)	1971, 1975, 1976
British Aircraft Corporation (BAC) Rapier	1971	IEI, Irano-British Dynamics[a] BAC (UK)	1976
Raytheon, MIM-23B Hawk, AIM-7F Sparrow, AIM-9G/H Sidewinder	1964	MIO/Westinghouse (USA)	

Sources: Various newspapers and periodicals.
[a]Partly foreign-owned.

Most of the projects involving imported weapons were limited to base-level maintenance on the part of Iran.[15] Little skill was required for most repairs of electronic equipment: Iranian technicians tested parts for defects and inserted imported replacements. The IEI's electro-optical division was managed by an American for many years.[16] By 1978, however, the proportion of U.S. engineers employed on the staff dropped from 40 to 4.5 percent according to the official record.

Aircraft. Iran Aircraft Industries (IACI) was created in 1970 as a joint venture between the government and the Northrop Corporation to perform maintenance and repair functions on military and civilian aircraft. The maintenance and repair facility was operated under contract by the Lockheed Aircraft Service Company and General Electric.[17] The IACI's operations grew rapidly during the 1970s and by the end of the decade it had opened facilities in five cities: Teheran, Esfahan, Bushehr, Shiraz, and Tabriz.

Plans for the expansion of the IACI's activities called for it to be producing parts and airframes and assembling light aircraft under license within twenty years. Iranian engineers there reportedly redesigned the leading-edge slats of the early McDonnell-Douglas F-4Es delivered to Iran, the same modification that was made on F-4Es delivered to Israel.

By 1977, three-quarters of the IACI's 2,600-person work force were Iranian. According to this author's interviews, Iranians were overrepresented in management and in unskilled jobs, whereas the skilled labor force included 600 workers from Pakistan, South Korea, and the Philippines and 50 technicians from the United States. The IACI's projections for its expansion estimated that a work force of 30,000 would be needed, including 3,250 engineers and 6,000 technicians.[18]

Several other projects were initiated in the aircraft sector during that period. As Table 4.2 shows, joint repair and assembly enterprises were contracted by Bell Helicopter (Textron and IHI), Grumman-Iran, and Norwasa (a jointly owned IACI/Northrop corporation). Bell Helicopter International agreed to sell Iran a turnkey overhaul facility for the helicopters that had been purchased for army aviation. Initially, Bell received a $255 million contract to train 1,500 pilots and 5,000 mechanics.[19] The implications of these projects for vocational training in Iran are discussed further in Chapter 9.

In 1978, Bell/IHI negotiated an agreement that stipulated the development and assembly of 4,400 Model 214ST helicopters by 1990, of which 3,800 would be sold to army aviation and 600 would be purchased by the government for resource development, maritime reconnaissance, and border patrol. Fifty percent of Bell's development costs for the 214ST were to be paid by Iran, in return for limited marketing rights once production began. The helicopter's T700/TIC engines and spare parts were made by General Electric.[20] Other U.S. manufacturers were to supply the avionics, instruments, hydraulic systems, bearings, and special materials. This was one of the largest projects to be canceled in 1979 as a result of the revolution.

Armored vehicles. The assembly of armored and military transport vehicles was more advanced than aircraft assembly. By 1970 Iran had a sizable automotive industry that was assembling vehicles for civilian and military use. Three foreign firms were producing military vehicles under license: Jeep Corporation (USA), British Leyland (U.K.), and Daimler-Benz (FRG). This was the only military industry in which private-sector Iranian manufacturers were involved.

Iran's M-47 and M-48 MBTs were retrofitted with diesel engines at an MIO plant in Dezful. Link belts for the tracks of several types of tanks were produced at Aligudarz, near Dorud. Iranian technicians were responsible for these facilities, producing foreign-designed equipment. The last contract to be approved before the revolution was for an Irano-British Dynamics plant in Esfahan to assemble Chieftain/Shir tanks. Negotiations were under way for the production of FRG Leopard I tanks, but they were not completed.

Communications. The transfer of communications technology and the production of communications equipment has become an important adjunct of military capability. The Shah invested in modern communications systems and expected Iranian technicians to be able to repair and eventually to produce some communications equipment. In 1974 military communications accounted for forty percent of the Iranian government's total investment in communications facilities (see Table 4.3)

In 1967, a contract for the Integrated National Telecommunications System was signed with a consortium of four companies, headed by Page Communications Engineers, a Northrop subsidiary. The single system was recommended by U.S. military advisers to consolidate five ongoing telecommunications projects. In 1975 the program was expanded under AT&T (USA). The U.S. Department of Defense estimated that $10 billion in telephone equipment would be sold to Iran for this project

TABLE 4.3

Capital Expenditures for Telecommunications
($U.S. millions)

Sector	1970	1974	1980 (est.)
Military:	57.3	143.1	240.0
Ministry of War, police, and Gendarmerie			
Civilian:	175.0	208.4	200.0
Telecommunications Company of Iran and Ministry of Post, Telephone and Telegraph			
% military of total	24.7	40.7	54.6

Source: U.S. Department of Commerce, Domestic and International Business Administration, *Iran: A Survey of U.S. Business Opportunities* (Washington, D.C.: U.S. Government Printing Office, 1977), p. 57.

alone. By 1979 Iranian technicians were undertaking replacement repairs in telephone equipment.

Research and development. Indigenous research and development was limited by the small number of scientific and technical personnel in Iran and by the scarcity of research facilities. One of the strategies used to overcome these limitations was to buy research and development directly, by financing research in other countries that would produce weapons that the Iranian government wanted (as was done with the Chieftain tank). Another was to buy training for Iranian engineers along with the weapons, as was done with the Bell helicopter. By the mid-1970s most weapons contracts that Iran concluded with foreign manufacturers provided opportunities for engineers and technicians to work alongside their foreign counterparts at in-country facilities, and to attend universities and technical institutes abroad.

The IEI, the Iran Advanced Technology Corporation (IATC), and the Center for Nuclear Research were created for the purpose of stimulating research and development. The IATC was established in the mid-1970s by Messerschmitt-Boelkow-Blohm (FRG) and the Iranian government. Iran controlled sixty-five percent of the corporation in the form of shares held by the National Iranian Oil Company, the Industrial Development and Renovation Organization, Bank Omran, and the Iranian air force's University of Science and Technology.[21] The purpose of the corporation was to encourage basic research in electronics and systems design and later in aeronautics and space design.

The Center for Nuclear Research was set up at Teheran University in 1959 with U.S. assistance when Iran became involved in the Eurodif Project. Aryamehr Technical University also had a research program that included military-related work.

The status of science and technology in Iran and other countries in the Middle East has been affected by the political climate. In most cases scientists work under strict political controls.[22] In response to Islamic politics, groups of scientists have begun to promote the concept of "Islamic science" in order to secure their positions. In theory, Iran's Islamic regime maintains the position that no fundamental incompatibility exists between religion and science, as long as science contributes to the well-being of the Islamic community. In practice, however, Western-trained scientists and engineers sometimes are considered politically suspect and find it difficult to find jobs. Historically, those who sought technological progress were criticized by some elements in the religious establishment and that kind of work was left to religious minorities.[23] The need for technical expertise during the war with Iraq and the large numbers of Iranians who were training in the decade preceding it probably moved Iran past this stage.

THE ORGANIZATION OF MILITARY ENTERPRISES

The projects described above were undertaken to improve Iran's short-term war-fighting capability and to enhance its military self-sufficiency in the long run. Whether or not they would contribute to the industrialization process in Iran was less important than were the military issues. The way in which the projects were handled indicates that their economic impact had a relatively low priority.

With very few exceptions, such as some construction materials and textiles, the private sector was not invited to participate in the military SOEs established during the 1970s. Loyalty to the Shah was at least as important as industrial management skills in choosing managers for the SOEs. Individuals who were close to the Court were selected to head the enterprises. Abolfath Mahvi, an entrepreneur who had a personal association with the Shah, was a central figure in the establishment of at least five of the military enterprises: the IACI, Irano-British Dynamics, Iran Marine Services, the Atomic Energy Organization, and ISIRAN.

Mahvi was not an industrial manager, but an intermediary between the Shah and foreign manufacturers. When he decided to sell his shares in ISIRAN, the Shah ordered the Plan and Budget Organization to buy them. Mahvi's explanation for the transfer was to improve security by transferring ISIRAN to the government. Whether or not this explained his reasons for selling, the question of security was raised in several situations.

In one such example, hand-held radios were to be produced for military use. The license for the radios was owned by General Electric. The matter was unclassified and General Electric officials thought that the production could easily have been undertaken by a private sector firm. Instead, the Shah elected to give IEI the contract because, according to those involved, he did not trust private producers. Thus, Admiral Ardalan managed nearly all the enterprises that were connected with electronics.

The Shah's nephew, Shahram, was a middleman in several other contracts to set up repair, maintenance, and production facilities, as was General Khatemi, a brother-in-law of the Shah. The entrepreneurial element in initiating the projects was part of the arms procurement decision-making process. General Khatemi's name was connected with payments made by U.S. aircraft manufacturers to smooth the way for sales contracts.[24] These characteristics of the military industrialization process in Iran have a great deal to do with the fact that the process was international, and suppliers were competing with one another for the contracts.

Supporters of the state-run enterprises argued that the SOEs could produce at lower costs. This was difficult to determine. MIO factories made copper wire and batteries to sell on the civilian market at lower prices than private manufacturers could offer. However, the MIO's accounts were not publicly available, so that there was no way of knowing what subsidies it might have received from the government treasury. Cooperation between the government and the private sector was not encouraged by competition from state factories. The Shah's lack of trust toward the private sector was reciprocated. United States military advisers recommended an integrated system to replace five separate telecommunications projects.

Within the government, there were likewise few opportunities for political involvement in military industries that might bring together investments in those projects with civilian investment plans. Several military SOEs had ministers of civilian departments on their boards of directors, but the boards met infrequently and were not policymaking groups. The board of Iran Electronics Industries had serving on it the minister of industry and mines, the finance minister, and the director of the Plan and Budget Organization and was chaired by General Toufanian. Other SOEs, including IHI and the IACI, operated directly under the authority of the MIO. In a third category were enterprises supervised by the MIO but funded as civilian enterprises: the battery factory at Parchin, the diesel motor plant, and military construction materials plants.[25] Military-related enterprises, like the Organization of Ports and Navigation, had no formal links to the military.

SUMMARY

Approaches that governments have taken to entering the arms production industry have varied widely. Taiwan chose, like Iran, to begin with technologically sophisticated weapons.[26] In contrast, the government of mainland China chose to begin by producing relatively outmoded weapons of Soviet design.[27] India has imported weapons of advanced design, produced weapons under license, and developed indigenous designs; the government's experience was that the cost of developing indigenous designs was higher than that of importing them.

All three of these countries are more industrialized than Iran, a characteristic that presumably increases the likelihood that arms production would stimulate domestic production in other industries.[28] Most of the new weapons facilities that were established in Iran resembled mirror-image "enclave industries," in which the production process was quite different from the majority of domestic industries, particularly in its use of advanced technology, but which (unlike enclave industries) produced for the domestic market rather than for export.

The history of arms production in Iran is a long one, with marked bursts of activity in the 1930s and again in the late 1960s. The incentive to produce arms domestically was to reduce Iran's financial and military/political dependence on foreign suppliers. Stimulating industrialization was a secondary matter. The time period of the latter effort was too short to evaluate how successful a policy of self-sufficiency can be in an industry of rapid technological change. Iran's technical capacity was increased; but, in the short term, setting up facilities to handle advanced weapons work increased Iran's dependence on imported technology rather than reducing it. However, at the end of the period, the military options were still whether to import advanced weapons or to do without them.

NOTES

1. Stockholm International Peace Research Institute, *World Armaments and Disarmament: SIPRI Yearbook 1979* (London: Taylor & Francis, 1979), p. 68.

2. Robert E. Harkavy, *The Arms Trade and the International System* (Cambridge, Mass.: Ballinger, 1979), p. 163.

3. Geoffrey Kemp, "Arms Transfers and the 'Back-End' Problems in Developing Countries," in Stephanie Neuman and Robert Harkavy, eds., *Arms Transfers in the Modern World* (New York: Praeger, 1980), p. 264.

4. Ulrich Albrecht, "Militarized Sub-Imperialism: The Case of Iran," in Mary Kaldor and Asbjorn Eide, eds., *The World Military Order* (London: Macmillan, 1979), p. 172.

5. Michael Moodie, "Defense Industries in the Third World: Problems and Promises," in Neuman and Harkavy, *Arms Transfers*, p. 302.

6. *Aviation Week and Space Technology*, June 2, 1975, p. 315.

7. Shahram Chubin, "Implications of the Military Buildup in Less Industrial States," in Uri Ra'anan et al., eds., *Arms Transfers to the Third World: The Military Buildup in Less Industrial Countries* (Boulder, Col.: Westview Press, 1978), p. 271.

8. Abrahamian, *Iran Between Two Revolutions*, p. 54.

9. This section is based on the history in Albrecht's "Militarized Sub-Imperialism."

10. F. Sadigh, *Impact of Government Policies on the Structure and Growth of Iranian Industry 1960-72* (London: Faculty of Economics, University of London, 1975), p. 167.

11. Peter Lock and Herbert Wulf, *Register of Arms Production in Developing Countries* (Hamburg: Study Group in Armaments and Underdevelopment, University of Hamburg, 1977), p. 76.

12. Since the revolution, Iran has acquired strategic surface-to-surface Soviet SCUD missiles from Libya.

13. H. Haftendorn, *Militarhilfe und Rustungsexporte der BRD* (Dusseldorf: Bertelsmann Universitats Verlag, 1971), p. 137.

14. Ownership was shared sixty-five percent and thirty-five percent, respectively.

15. Base-level maintenance functions are described by Stephanie Neuman in *Unravelling the Triad: Arms Transfers, Indigenous Defense Production, and Dependency—Iran as an Example* (Washington, D.C.: Foreign Affairs Research Documentation Center, Department of State, 1979), p. 20.

16. *New York Times*, September 22, 1975.

17. Neuman, *Unravelling the Triad*, p. 17. Neuman's study provides the most thorough information available to the public on the IACI.

18. Ibid., p. 24.

19. *Aviation Week and Space Technology*, June 2, 1975, p. 309.

20. Interavia, *Airletter* 8395, December 4, 1975.

21. *Aviation Week and Space Technology*, August 7, 1978.

22. Martin Rudner, "Higher Education and the Development of Science in Islamic Countries: A Comparative Analysis," *Canadian Journal of Development Studies* 4, 1 (1983): 63-94.

23. Ibid.

24. *Washington Post*, January 27, 1980.

25. This information is based on research undertaken by Ms. Jaleh Amin in 1979-1980.

26. Neuman, *Unravelling the Triad*, p. 27.

27. Harlan W. Jencks, "The Chinese 'Military-Industrial Complex' and Defense Modernization," *Asian Survey*, 20, 10 (October 1980): 968.

28. David K. Whynes, *The Economics of Third World Military Expenditures* (Austin: University of Texas Press, 1979).

FIVE

Military Expenditures and Foreign Debt

Nearly all the weapons and military technology acquired by the governments of less industrial countries have been supplied through the arms trade rather than by domestic production. In the 1970s the arms trade spiraled; by 1976 weapons accounted for forty-three percent of the value of all imports by developing countries ($11.2 billion out of $26 billion),[1] and two years later the bill for arms imports had risen to $15.6 billion.

Foreign indebtedness paralleled the growth of trade in weapons. Policymakers and planners shifted their attention from domestic constraints on economic growth to "the financial basis of development."[2] The governments of many countries reacted to the need for foreign exchange by shifting resources into producing goods for export rather than for domestic consumption. Eventually, by the 1980s, foreign exchange shortages began to act as a brake on arms imports. But this did not occur until after other adjustments had been tried.

The problem was exacerbated by the demand for imports from industries. The most rapidly industrializing countries were the heaviest foreign borrowers and the biggest military spenders. And further contributing to the situation was the tendency of many governments to respond to the political pressures that accompanied industrialization with populist policies that raised the countries' import bills even more.[3]

Despite Iran's abundant oil resources, foreign exchange pressures were felt there as well. This chapter discusses the role played by arms imports in Iran's foreign indebtedness. From a historical perspective, buying arms from abroad has had an important impact on Iran's foreign

67

exchange position, but is just one dimension of a political economy that fosters indebtedness.

IDENTIFYING MILITARY DEBTS

Some of Iran's foreign borrowing was directly linked to weapons imports. How much of Iran's arms imports at any given time were purchased through foreign borrowing is not known, however, with the exception of a few years when there was no public borrowing. Income from foreign loans was not itemized in the military budget; only repayments were recorded. Without knowing the amount of the terms of repayment, these figures could not be used to estimate the total debt.

Specific loans are described in secondary sources. In 1969 a loan for $328 million to finance arms purchases was taken out by the Iranian government.[4] It was reported in the press, but it was not identified in the government budget, although it amounted to nearly half of the Ministry of War's total budget for that year. Another loan of $500 million was made to the Iranian government by Chase Manhattan Bank in 1977 to help the government meet "unchecked military expenditures."[5] Loans to the SOEs to finance imports were handled in the same manner. For example, a loan from the French government to pay for two French nuclear reactors did not appear in the published budget of the Iran Atomic Energy Organization.

Private loans and credits that financed military purchases were even more difficult to document than public ones. Various financial arrangements were made by the Iranian government to purchase foreign arms. Oil supplies were bartered for armaments, which presumably did not involve credits. The government of Iran was permitted to buy arms "on time." Four British Vosper-Throneycroft destroyers, for example, were paid for in installments, the first installment being a loan from a British bank consortium. The Organization of Ports and Navigation received credit for the construction of the Chahbahar naval base by private British construction firms through an oil barter arrangement with British Shell. Private arrangements of this kind increased in the aftermath of the oil boom.

TRENDS IN MILITARY SPENDING AND FOREIGN DEBTS

The Qajars regularly used foreign loans to defray the costs of military expenditures. Reza Shah, however, was reluctant to do so. In 1937 the United States offered to provide military credits to Iran and the offer was declined. Then, after World War II, the practice was resumed again. In 1948 the United States extended $17 million in credit to Iran for the purchase of surplus U.S. military equipment. By 1970 U.S. military assistance, which included grant and loan aid, had accumulated to over half a billion dollars (Table 5.1). Over half of the grant and loan aid that the United States extended to Iran from 1945 to 1966 was for military purposes.[6]

In 1969, U.S. military aid to Iran began to decline. It was already being replaced by Export-Import Bank loans. These were low (noncommercial) interest loans that were to be spent on military purchases from the United States (Table 5.2).[7] By 1966 Iran owed the bank a total of $210 million for nonmilitary purchases, its largest outstanding debt.[8] In the four years from 1970 to 1974, Iran borrowed a total of $620 million for military expenditures.

From the standpoint of the role of arms exports in U.S. policy, it is worthy of note that military loans were not part of the bank's original mandate from Congress; the bank was created for the purpose of encouraging private enterprise abroad by making loans to foreign enterprises which had a proven profit-making ability. But when arms sales came to be seen as a means of leverage in foreign policy as well as a source of foreign exchange, they were treated like any other export commodity and loans were made to governments, too. During the mid-1960s, the bank was lending almost half of its funds for military purchases. In 1970 a specific restriction was placed on the bank, prohibiting it from making loans for military purchases to "developing countries," but that excluded Iran with its relatively high per capita income.[9]

During the 1970s Iran spent a larger proportion of its foreign exchange on arms imports than did the governments of most other countries, particularly those outside the Middle East. Data published by the U.S. Agency for International Development show that from 1974 to 1978, Iran and Iraq both imported military goods and services valued at about twenty-two percent of total imports.[10] In contrast, India used ten percent

TABLE 5.1

U.S. Military Assistance and Military Sales to Iran
($U.S. millions)

Years	Military assistance programs	Foreign military sales (deliveries)
1950-1964/65	391.6	—
1965/66	40.0	—
1966/67	93.5	—
1967/68	75.4	—
1968/69	85.8	—
1969/70	45.3	231.8
1970/71	12.8	127.7
1971/72	4.3	78.6
1972/73	6.3	214.8
1973/74	2.6	245.3
1974/75	.2	648.6
1975/76	negligible	1,000.1
1976/77	—	1,924.9
1977/78	—	2,424.7
1978/79	—	1,907.4
1979/80	—	924.5
Total		9,740.3

Sources: SIPRI Yearbook and CIA, Handbook of Economic Statistics, 1980.

TABLE 5.2

Eximbank Loans to Iran
(U.S. dollars)

Years	Military equipment and services	Total credit	Total transactions including insurance
1966/67	—	94,700	113,177,100
1968/69	—	29,790,000	38,949,518
1969/70	—	7,192,804	40,736,717
1970/71	120,000,000	188,151,001	295,863,187
1971/72	100,000,000	32,677,661	234,507,780
1972/73	200,000,000	239,873,679	517,996,754
1973/74	200,000,000	266,713,111	319,827,998
1974/75	—	5,693,963	
1975/76			127,698,627
1976/77			
1977/78		17,850,000	42,731,217

Source: U.S. Export-Import Bank, Annual Report, various years. The Reports stopped providing specific country data from 1975 on.

of its foreign exchange for military imports.[11] The 1978 average for sub-Saharan African countries was approximately 9.3 percent.[12]

This was a new situation for Iran. The military's share in Iran's total imports quadrupled during the decade from 1964 to 1974.[13] Military imports also increased as a proportion of machinery and transport imports. In the 1970s, the military spent well over half of its procurement funds and at least half of its total military budget abroad (Table 5.3). In light of what we know about Iran's arms imports bill and the lack of reliable documentation of arms imports (see Chapter 3), it is possible that as much as eighty percent of military expenditures in those years may have been spent abroad.

Data on Iran's total indebtedness do not distinguish between military and civilian loans. In effect, the distinction is not important. Loans made to the government for civilian purposes free foreign exchange reserves for present military purchases. Looking at the trends in public indebtedness for Iran, military expenditures and arms imports do not appear to have had a notable effect on how much the government borrowed from abroad. Table 5.4 shows that in the 1950s, public debt increased more rapidly than military spending. In other words, pressures other than military spending drove debt levels up during that period.

Over the ten years from 1968 to 1977, the pattern was reversed: military spending grew faster than did indebtedness. In fact, with the oil price increases, the government was able to liquidate some of its debts. This situation came to an end in the year before the revolution. The 1978/79 budget had a deficit, which was to be covered partially by $4 billion in foreign borrowing and almost the equivalent in domestic borrowing and reductions in planned expenditures.

NONMILITARY CAUSES OF INDEBTEDNESS

The lack of a direct variance between levels of military spending and foreign indebtedness indicates that other factors are involved in the explanation of foreign borrowing. Nor is it sufficient to attribute borrowing prior to the oil boom to a shortage of funds. It was the government, not the private sector, that incurred the most foreign debts. Why Iran's rulers used foreign loans to finance the state is a more general question of political economy.

TABLE 5.3

Expenditures and Arms Imports
($U.S. millions)

Year	Military budget	Arms imports	Procurement budget	Arms imports as a percentage of military budget	Arms imports as a percentage of procurement budget
1971	2,505	320	480.7	12.8	66.6
1973	3,720	525	929.9	14.1	56.5
1975	8,646	1,200	4,637.0	13.9	25.9
1977	8,747	2,400	4,561.1	27.4	52.6

Sources: Military expenditure figures in this table are taken from official Iranian budgets. The official figures are underestimates. The procurement budget figures used here are a composite of the official procurement budget and of the "special activities" category which reportedly was spent on arms procurement. Arms imports figures are from U.S. ACDA reports.

TABLE 5.4

Foreign Debts and Military Expenditures
(average annual percentage of increase)

	1948-57	1958-67	1968-77
Outstanding public debt (disbursed)	88.7	13.2	46.2
Military budget	24.2	17.8	142.7

Sources: Public debt figures from 1958 on are taken from the World Bank series, and those from before then from the *Statesmen's Yearbook* and data compiled by the Department of Overseas Trade, Great Britain. Military budget figures are official Iranian budget estimates, which include the Gendarmerie and police.

First, to the extent that Iran's economy in the nineteenth century was integrated at all above the level of local and largely self-sufficient communities, it was oriented outward toward foreign markets. Cotton farmers in northern Iran were dependent on Russian markets for their raw cotton in the absence of a domestic textile industry. In southern Iran, people found it more economical to import rice than to buy that grown near the Caspian Sea in the north because domestic transportation networks were poor.[14] With trade such an important economic activity, customs receipts were a main source of revenue for the government. Thus, government finances were directly linked to foreign economic transactions.

A second consideration that reinforced the impact of international factors on government was the extraordinary military and political interest that foreign powers took in Iran, which has been discussed in previous chapters. The agreement that Russia and Britain reached in 1907 over their respective spheres of influence in Iran was an example of the state's lack of control over the country, which affected its ability to enforce all sorts of measures including the collection of revenue. The competition among foreign governments for influence in Iran also meant that foreign loans were made available as instruments of that influence.

During the constitutional revolution (1907-1909), those who tried to set up a new basis for governing saw foreign borrowing as a fundamental attribute of the Qajar regime that they opposed and they attempted to raise money through public subscriptions to pay off the debts. Although this failed, the parliament refused to accept an Anglo-Russian loan offer in 1909.[15] In 1919, a second British offer failed to receive parliamentary approval.

The unstable political situation within Iran made it difficult to prevent officials from continuing to borrow money from willing lenders. Despite the political controversy that foreign borrowing provoked, in 1920 the treasury's debts, owed mainly to the British Imperial Bank of Persia, amounted to more than half of Iran's export receipts. In 1921 the government that replaced the Qajars hired an American financial adviser, Arthur Millspaugh, to reorganize public finances. When Millspaugh recommended that the government reduce military spending among other measures, it led to his dismissal. But eventually both Iran's debts and military spending were reduced in the context of Reza Shah's tight hold on politics.

After World War II, foreign debts again increased. Iran's economy was not prospering, the government had taken on a commitment to formal development planning, and foreign lenders (mainly the United States) were interested in building influence there. Many of the loans that were made were to finance the economic plans. The First Plan was launched in 1947, with nearly one-third of the disbursements made under it coming from foreign loans. During the Second Plan foreign borrowing also increased; in fact, foreign financing was so crucial that waiting to conclude negotiations on foreign loans often delayed the announcement of the government's annual budget.

The Third Plan (1963-1967) was an exception. When it was initiated, Iran was in the midst of a recession. Yet it was a conservative plan, that emphasized balanced growth rather than large capital investments. Comparatively, Iran was less reliant on foreign credit during that period than were other less industrial countries.[16] The inflow of foreign capital during the Third Plan represented 2.5 percent of the GNP, in contrast with an average of 3.5 percent for all developing countries.

The large-scale infrastructure and industrial projects initiated during the Fourth Plan (1968-1972) required more foreign exchange. The beginning of the plan coincided with the buildup in advanced weapon imports. By 1970, halfway through the plan, nearly three-quarters of the country's $3 billion foreign debt was owned by the government. The largest borrowers were the National Petrochemical Company ($630 million), the National Iranian Gas Company ($300 million), and the National Telecommunications Company ($250 million).

In addition to long-term loans like those from the Export-Import Bank, the government acquired a variety of short-term obligations to meet its liquidity needs and operating expenses. Parliament tried to proscribe the use of foreign loans for current expenditures by appending a prohibition to the Fourth Plan;[17] but there were many ways of circumventing this. One was to use loans to finance state enterprises and shift their funding to the ordinary government budget. This may account for a small portion of the foreign debt obligations of the SOEs.

On other occasions, the prohibition seems to have been simply ignored. For example, in 1970 the government borrowed $19.6 million to help cover a $58 million deficit. (In most such cases, the government did not identify the lender.) When Iran's current account surplus fell from $12 billion to $5 billion between 1974 and 1977, the government adopted a policy of maintaining sizable deposits in foreign banks and using foreign loans for current expenditures. These deposits were held in the form of "call money," which earned a rate of interest about one and a half percent lower than the interest rates at which the government was borrowing.

After the Fourth Plan, when Iran's oil revenues had increased thereby improving its financial outlook, syndicated private bank loans became more common. From 1973 to 1978, the Fifth Plan period, syndicated loans were made to the government and to the private sector in approximately equal proportions: $2.9 billion to the government, and $2 billion to the private sector. The amount of private sector debt is one indication of changes that were taking place in Iran's economy, in which there were enterprises of sufficient size to be interested in the international capital market.

Subsidiaries of multinationals operating in Iran accumulated substantial foreign debts, too. A number of the foreign loans acquired by Iran during the 1970s actually were credits extended by parent firms to their subsidiaries in Iran. One example was the $1 billion credit line established by the Ex-Im Bank of Japan for a joint Japanese-Iranian petrochemical project in southern Bandar Shahpur.[18]

TRADE ADJUSTMENT AND MONETARY STABILIZATION

Despite the fact that for Iran and other developing countries military imports consume a large share of the foreign exchange available, the question of how arms imports are taken into account in trade adjustment policies has received little attention.[19] Several IMF stabilization programs have specifically included reducing military expenditures as one of the stipulations for assistance.[20] However, few secondary analyses of stabilization policy refer either to military spending or to the arms trade.[21]

Military imports can contribute to inflation as well as to foreign trade deficits. First, they consume scarce foreign exchange that might otherwise be used for intermediate and capital goods that would expand domestic production. Second, they compete for foreign exchange with consumer goods imports and thereby push up domestic consumer prices. Iran's trade figures illustrate these processes. Intermediate and capital goods imports increased, along with arms imports, in the 1970s in response to increased demand from military and civilian industries. And, Iran's consumer goods imports declined when arms imports began to rise significantly. From 1963 to 1969, consumer goods dropped from twenty-five percent of total imports to ten percent.

Inflation did not become a serious problem in postwar Iran until the 1970s. Official figures put the rates of inflation at two percent in 1970 and 19.8 percent in 1974.[22] According to IMF estimates, the inflation rate was higher than that: 14.5 percent in 1971, rising to 27.7 percent in 1974. An Iranian economist noted the correspondence of inflation trends to oil revenues, which increased buying power but not productive capacity.[23] The prices of many of the goods that Iran was importing were also increasing and contributing to domestic inflationary pressures.

In 1973-74, the price of oil rose enough to support a 287 percent increase in government expenditures and a 42 percent increase in the liquidity of the private sector.[24] Several Iranian economists recommended selling less oil and keeping closer control over the ministries' funding requests, particularly military spending. In the midst of the oil boom, the ministries' budgets represented "wish lists" for programs that they could not necessarily carry out.

The Fifth Plan was revised on the basis of the higher oil revenues. But, almost as soon as the revision was completed, oil prices stopped their steady climb. Consequently, the figures in the plan overestimated revenues and when they did not match the estimates, many development projects that had been begun could not be finished. In one region, this author saw schools and technical institutes that had been started and then stopped before completion. Involuntary fiscal restraints were operating. According to an investment banker who spent those years in Teheran, cutting off funds for development projects cost the Shah the support of the ministry officials and private contractors who were involved with those projects.

Inflation that is linked to foreign trade creates a particularly difficult problem for domestic authorities. Central Bank officials complained that they had too little authority over the money supply to deal effectively with the inflation. The measures that were taken were decided on at the highest levels and were directed toward specific groups and types of expenditures. The Shah acknowledged the problem, declaring that the "bankruptcy was worse than [military] defeat." An imperial commission was established in 1976 to monitor development expenditures and "eliminate waste." When Jamshid Amuzegar was appointed prime minister a year later, he promised to "take a close look at those government programs that do not contribute to production."[25]

But there was no public reference to the high cost of military imports. Although a few military orders were postponed, others were added, including a $4 billion order for 250 F-18s. From 1974 on, expenditures on weapons imports increased from four percent of trade receipts to approximately nine percent (Table 5.5). Standing agreements for military purchases from abroad gave an impetus to maintain those expenditures that could not readily be curbed.

The Shah was reluctant to place the burden on consumers. Tariffs on certain categories of imported consumer goods were reduced. The Ministry of Economy and Finance introduced a plan for substantial increases in taxation that would raise the share of tax revenues in the budget from around 13 percent to 35 percent.[26] Politically, the timing was bad. The clergy were courting supporters in the bazaar by promising to eliminate taxes if they gained control of the government.

Instead, a series of restrictive policies and political recriminations surrounding the inflation focused on the private sector, which received some of the blame for the problem. Price controls and "antiprofiteering" measures were introduced. Several prominent industrialists were arrested for violating price control regulations. The government's hectic ef-

TABLE 5.5

Foreign Trade Receipts and Arms Imports
(in $U.S. millions)

Year	Exports of goods and nonfactor services	Arms imports	Percent arms imports of trade receipts
1963	1,140.7	27.0	2.4
1964	1,188.0	26.0	2.2
1965	1,347.0	34.0	2.5
1966	1,478.0	56.0	3.8
1967	1,176.0	104.0	8.8
1968	1,325.0	140.0	10.6
1969	1,602.0	220.0	13.7
1970	2,603.0	160.0	6.1
1971	3,946.0	320.0	8.1
1972	4,269.0	525.0	12.3
1973	6,720.0	525.0	7.8
1974	22,315.0	1,000.0	4.5
1975	22,201.9	1,200.0	5.4
1976	26,143.0	2,400.0	9.2
1977	27,315.3	2,400.0	8.8
1978		2,100.0	
1979			
1980			

Sources: International Monetary Fund, *Balance of Payments Year Book*, various years, and ACDA, *World Military Expenditures and Arms Trade*.

forts to curb the inflation with punitive measures may have encouraged the flight of private capital from the country, which was then already gaining momentum.

Stabilization measures would be a political quagmire as long as imports remained at high levels and domestic production did not increase. Firouz Vakil estimated the value of nonoil exports that would have to be produced to cover the projected demand for imports, including arms. By 1992, Iran would need to raise from $39.7 to $56.7 billion to support a target GNP of $283.7 billion.[27] This is compared to actual nonoil export earnings of $959 million in 1973. Reaching the required level of earning would have meant achieving a growth rate of approximately seven hundred percent annually.

SUMMARY

Arising primarily from government borrowing, Iran's foreign debts were a product of a generalized and long-term political fragility. The combination of the state's tenuous hold over the country, its position in the midst of competition among more powerful countries, and, later, its oil resources encouraged its rulers to look outward for revenues as well as for military support. In their weakness, the last Qajars sought loans from Britain and Russia as an alternative to domestic revenues. After Reza Shah had consolidated the state's power over alternative sources of finance, the government relied less on foreign debts.

Foreign borrowing rose once again after World War II, reaching a high point in the late 1960s and shifting from official to commercial loans. Still uncertain of his domestic support, the Shah nonetheless adopted military and development policies that required high-technology imports. Military expenditures were clearly not the only cause of Iran's trade adjustment problems and indebtedness; however, they were a factor. Compared to other less industrial countries, Iran used a high proportion of its foreign exchange on weapons imports, as did Iraq, its chief military rival.

During the brief period when Iran's foreign exchange earnings increased so rapidly, the competition for foreign exchange was not serious. After oil revenues leveled off, however, the continued high expenditures on arms imports were compensated for by new foreign borrowing in addition to cutbacks in development projects and attempts to place controls on the private sector. Without the option of borrowing, the cutbacks in development projects could have been more severe.

One of the policy implications of Iran's experience is that using military funds to finance imports may have important political costs that derive from their economic effects. Expected gains in military security derived from importing weapons may be offset by the attendant restrictions on using foreign exchange for other purposes. This is particularly true when foreign borrowing and military dependence is as politically unpopular as it has been in Iran. Many of Iran's rulers have used foreign loans to finance military imports and most of them lost political support as a result.

NOTES

1. Ruth Leger Sivard, *World Military and Social Expenditures 1980* (Leesburg, Va.: World Priorities, 1980), p. 20.

2. Emma Rothschild, "Banks: The Politics of Debt," *New York Review of Books*, June 24, 1976.

3. Carlos F. Diaz-Alejandro, "Southern Core Stabilization Plans," in William R. Cline and Sidney Weintraub, eds., *Economic Stabilization in Developing Countries* (Washington, D.C.: Brookings Institution, 1981), p. 222.

4. Economist Intelligence Unit, *Quarterly Economic Review*, Economic Review of Iran, 1969, p. 5.

5. *The Economist* (London), February 21, 1979.

6. Marvin Zonis, *The Political Elite of Iran* (Princeton: Princeton University Press, 1971), p. 109, from U.S. Office of Statistics and Reports, International Cooperation Administration, *Foreign Assistance and Assistance From International Organizations, July 1, 1945 to June 30, 1966* (Washington, D.C.: U.S. Government Printing Office, 1967), p. 12.

7. Interest rates varied from 4.5 to 5.5 percent in 1966, and rose to about 6 percent in 1984. Interest charges were divided between the Iranian government and the U.S. Department of Defense.

8. *New York Times*, July 31, 1967.

9. U.S. Government Accounting Office, *Audit of the Export-Import Bank of the United States*, Report to Congress by the Comptroller General of the United States (Washington, D.C.: U.S. Government Printing Office, 1972), p. 9.

10. U.S. Agency for International Development, *Economic Development Versus Military Expenditures in Countries Receiving U.S. Aid: Priorities and Competition for Resources*, Report submitted to the Committees on Foreign Affairs and Foreign Relations (Washington, D.C.: U.S. Government Printing Office, 1980), p. 49.

11. Onkar Marwah, "India's Military Power and Policy," in Onkar Marwah and Jonathan Pollack, eds., *Military Power in Asian States* (Boulder, Col.: Westview Press, 1980), p. 124.

12. Lance Taylor, "The Costly Arms Trade," *New York Times*, December 22, 1981.

13. Peter Lock and Herbert Wulf, "The Economic Consequences of the Transfer of Military-Oriented Technology," in Mary Kaldor and Ashbjorn Eide, eds., *The World Military Order: The Impact of Military Technology on the Third World* (New York: Praeger, 1979), p. 215.

14. Julian Bharier, *Economic Development in Iran, 1900-1970* (New York: Oxford University Press, 1971), p. 109.

15. Peter Avery, *Modern Iran* (New York: Praeger, 1965), p. 141.

16. Jahangir Amuzegar and M. Ali Fekrat, *Iran: Economic Development Under Dualistic Conditions* (Chicago: University of Chicago Press, 1971), p. 63.

17. Economist Intelligence Unit, *Quarterly Economic Review*, Economic Review of Iran, 1968.

18. The Bank of Japan was concerned about the project's soaring costs and insisted that the Iranian National Petrochemical Company guarantee the full amount of the bank's investment. *AMPO* (Tokyo, 1978).

19. An exception is P. Terhal, "Guns or Grain: Macro-Economic Costs of Indian Defense, 1969-70," *Economic and Political Weekly* (Bombay) 16, 49 (December 5, 1981): 1995-2004. Terhal discusses the effects of India's military imports on its balance of payments and investment.

20. The IMF recommended that the government of Morocco reduce military expenditures in 1981.

21. Examples of studies that would have been more realistic had they included reference to the arms trade are: William R. Cline et al., *World Inflation and the Developing Countries* (Washington, D.C.: Brookings Institution, 1980); William R. Cline and Sidney Weintraub, eds., *Economic Stabilization in the Developing Countries* (Washington, D.C.: Brookings Institution, 1981); Cheryl Payer, *The Debt Trap* (New York: Monthly Review Press, 1974).

22. Firouz Vakil, "Iran's Basic Macroeconomic Problems: A Twenty-Year Horizon," *Economic Development and Cultural Change* 25, 4 (July 1977): 721.

23. Ibid., p. 722.

24. Hossein Razavi and Firouz Vakil, *The Political Environment of Economic Planning in Iran* (Boulder, Col.: Westview Press, 1984), p. 80.

25. Economist Intelligence Unit, *Quarterly Economic Review*, Economic Review of Iran, 1975.

26. Ibid., 1977.

27. Vakil, "Iran's Basic Macroeconomic Problems," p. 728.

SIX

Economic Growth and Development

By 1974, Iran was well on the way to becoming a significant regional military power. As we have seen, its armed forces were fighting a counter-insurgency war in Oman, the Iranian navy was patrolling the Gulf and beyond, and its arsenal of modern weapons was growing rapidly. The country's oil wealth temporarily obscured the urgent dual pressures of population and food that were forcing other governments to weigh military and other expenditures against the staggering foreign debts that they were accumulating.

Even during the oil boom, however, both the Shah and Iranian economic planners realized that the country's oil reserves were finite and sustained economic growth would eventually require alternative sources of investment capital and foreign exchange. Without these changes, the inability to maintain intermediate and capital goods imports would force the postponement of domestic economic growth. The next four chapters discuss how military expenditures fit into this picture.

EARLIER RESEARCH ON IRAN

Four previously published articles specifically addressed the question of Iranian military expenditures and the country's prospects for growth and development. Each approached the problem from a somewhat different perspective. The first, by Manoucher Parvin, was published in 1968,[1] and was essentially a plea to the Shah to reallocate resources from the military sector to development programs that would improve the quality of life for impoverished Iranians. Yet, for almost a decade after Parvin's state-

83

ment was published, "guns-or-butter" issues in the Iranian economy received virtually no attention in academic literature or in the publications of practitioners interested in Iran's development problems.

During and after the 1978-1979 revolution, three additional articles on military expenditures were published. Two of them paid particular attention to the weaknesses in Iran's military spending data and economic indicators.[2] Theodore Moran went on to discuss alternative uses for funds that had been invested in the military; the three areas in which he thought government funds were most needed were rural and urban development and employment. He maintained that military power had been emphasized too much during the 1970s, to the detriment of development. The other article, by Stephanie Neuman, primarily addressed the methodological and conceptual pitfalls to which economic impact analysis is susceptible rather than the Iranian economy itself. She was particularly critical of the reliance on macroeconomic data and the failure to distinguish what goods and services are actually purchased from military budgets.

Neuman's description of the issue as being clouded by polemics, as opposed to empirically grounded theory, is discussed at greater length in a recent comparative study of military spending by Nicole Ball.[3] Ball's review of the theoretical state of the field suggests that we are a long way from having a general analytical model equal to the problem of estimating the impact of military spending on growth and development. Not only is there disagreement about how growth and development occur, but it also is unwise to generalize about the effects of military spending on economies that are very different in structure.

In addition, military spending differs in substance from one country to another, as does the implementation of military policies through which those funds are spent. And, still less tangibly, the political character of military policy can also be assumed to differ from one country to the next. People's attitudes about their governments' military policies, to take one example, apparently influence their willingness to participate in the "military economy." Profound differences over military policy can discourage entrepreneurs from responding to incentives to participate in military projects or, conversely, discourage the government from permitting private sector participation in such projects.

This kind of detailed contextual analysis still remains to be done. The only two other studies of military spending that touched on Iran were comparative and used macroeconomic data. Robert Looney's study of Iran's military spending was one that used comparative economic analysis, based on Emile Benoit's model with the addition of an intermediate variable—resource endowment.[4] Although Looney included a short discussion of Iran's specific economic situation, the formal data analysis was based on groupings of countries by region, with Iran placed together with other oil-producing countries of the Middle East. In actuality, Iran's economic environment and performance are different from most of the other oil-producing countries in a number of respects, such as the existence of nonoil resources, a large and rapidly growing population, and an existing industrial capacity.

Looney's data analysis showed that countries like Iran, with a rich endowment of natural resources (primarily oil), experienced relatively fewer negative effects from high levels of military expenditures than resource-poor countries. Wassily Leontief and Faye Duchin reached the same conclusion when they included Iran in projections of different levels and compositions of military spending through a global input-output model.[5] This is not a surprising conclusion; but, more important, it does not prepare us for the economic slowdown that began in Iran in the mid-1970s, a slowdown that was partly related to the fact that Iran's more complex and developed economy was more sensitive to dislocations caused by profound changes in government spending patterns, including military spending, whereas more oil-centered economies were less sensitive.

ECONOMIC GROWTH PERFORMANCE

Compared with the rates of economic growth achieved by other countries, including oil-producing countries, the performance of Iran's economy during the 1960s and 1970s was favorable. From 1960 to 1972, Iran's rate of growth equaled Japan's and was surpassed only by those of Libya and Taiwan.[6] Per capita, only eight countries in the world had *national income* growth rates higher than that of Iran, which stood at 6.3 percent. From 1970 to 1978, the average *GDP* growth rate for all capital-surplus oil-exporting countries was 5.6 percent;[7] Iran's was 7.8 percent from 1970 to 1977.

A comparison of the rate of growth in military spending in Iran and the rate of growth of Iran's GDP does not provide any clear evidence that military spending had a negative economic impact (Table 6.1), if one uses an arbitrary, undiscriminating criterion such as a low or negative growth rate. In fact, from 1965 to 1970, when Iran's military spending was growing rapidly, the real rate of growth in Iran's GDP also increased. During the 1970-1977 period, the rate of growth in military spending declined very slightly and GDP growth rates evidenced no increase.

Comparing economic and military spending data in this way, however, oversimplifies both the process of economic growth and the composition of military spending. The juxtaposition of military spending and GDP data for the same time periods, as presented in Table 6.1, is not realistic in terms of the time that is needed for a series of complex economic interactions to occur and for the impact of military spending to be felt. Savings and investment decisions, for example, are influenced by a variety of factors including previously realized returns on investment, interest and taxation rates, external economies (actual or anticipated), and the investment "climate," the confidence that potential investors have in future economic growth—each of which may, in turn, be affected by military spending. The interplay of these factors is likely to take place over a longer period of time than one or two years.

Emile Benoit undertook what he called a "lead-lag" analysis, but unfortunately did not report on what procedure he used nor the results of the analysis, other than to state that he could not tell whether changes in military expenditures came before changes in economic growth rates or after them.[8] That is an important caution; correlation never proves the direction of causation. Causation can be better understood if we look at specific situations.

A case in point is his finding that military spending and growth were positively correlated *when* foreign capital was available to the government at "concessionary" rates. Egypt was one of the countries to which this condition applied and which Benoit selected for a case study. And, during the period that Soviet military assistance was available, the Egyptian economy experienced positive economic growth while it maintained high levels of military spending.

However, a later study of Egyptian military spending showed that the long-term costs of military spending were higher despite the aid.[9]

TABLE 6.1

Growth Rates for GDP and Military Expenditures

Years	GDP[a] %	National defense[b] %
1955-60	15.3	12.2
1960-65	11.1	19.2
1965-70	16.1	43.0
1970-75	7.5	37.5
1975-77	6.9	-10.3
1978-83	- .5	

Sources: GDP figures are from *World Tables 1980*, pp. 106-107, and *Worldwide Economic Indicators: Annual Comparative Statistics for 131 Countries With World and Regional Reports*, 1985 ed. (New York: Business International Corporation, 1985), pp. 104-105. National defense expenditures are from government budgets.
[a]Average annual real growth rates in 1974 prices.
[b]Average annual real growth rates in 1975 prices.

Soviet military assistance was to be repaid over eleven years, from 1959 to 1970. During that period the Egyptian government found it necessary to draw on its foreign exchange reserves, depleting them by *sixty percent*. Since then, Egypt's military spending has continued to rise and its foreign debts have risen too.

In Iran's case, time also appears to make a difference in findings on the impact of military expenditures on growth. When a time lag was introduced to allow for a delayed response to military spending, the outcome was less positive than when the comparison was between spending and performance in concurrent periods (Figure 6.1). With the exception of 1970-1977, the points from which the trend lines in the figure were constructed represent average rates of growth over a five-year period, as they did in Table 6.1. But in this case, the military spending figures are for period "t" and those for economic growth are for period "t+1." Thus, from 1955 to 1960, military expenditures increased at an average annual rate of 12.2 percent and, in the subsequent period, the GDP growth rate fell to 7.5 percent.

With the time lag included, the gap between GDP growth rates and the rate of growth in military spending widened. Economic growth

With respect to budgetary decisions, it is important to remember that in the oil-producing countries, resources shifted from the military sector would remain in the public sector rather than reverting to the private sector. How productively these resources would be used would depend on the politics involved as well as on economic considerations, such as the availability of profitable opportunities for investment in civilian activities (the absorptive capacity of the economy). In Iran, such resources could have found their way into any of the following areas: state enterprises (SOEs), birth control programs, food and other consumer goods subsidies, or government operating costs, including corruption, and others.[11] The productivity of investments in civilian programs would only have been greater if they had contributed to, for example, a healthier and more educated population than if they were used to underwrite poorly run SOEs whose managers were immune from financial oversight.

INVESTMENT AND CAPITAL FORMATION

Another way of assessing economic impact is to look at trends in investment and capital formation. Private sector investment is of particular interest, because Iran had and continues to have a mixed economy. One of the challenges for development was to provide incentives that would bring private financial capital into the economy. Historically, finances have been privately held within families and the capital has not always found its way into productive investments. Because the creation of financial markets has been a central issue in development planning, the relationship between private capital formation and military spending, if any, needs to be examined.

Looking specifically at rates of investment, military expenditures did not appear to have a discernible negative impact, but the opposite. Capital formation data, published by the Central Bank, show that private investment rates remained at high levels throughout the period (Table 6.2). Private capital formation as a percentage of GNP increased from 1971 to 1975, after a small decline during the previous four years. When a time lag was introduced, the result showed that a relatively low rate of growth in military spending was followed by a decline in private capital formation. Conversely, a high level of military spending was followed by an increase in private capital formation.

TABLE 6.2

Private Gross Domestic Fixed Capital Formation
(in billions of constant rials)

	1963[a]	1967[a]	1971[a]	1975[b]
Private GDFCF	32.5	58	77.7	410.5
Percentage of GNP	8.5	11.3	10.0	12.6
Percentage of total GDFCF	64.6	51.3	43.0	42.0

[a]Firouz Tofiq, "Development of Iran: A Statistical Note," in Jane W. Jacqz, ed., *Iran: Past, Present and Future* (New York: Aspen Institute for Humanistic Studies, 1976), p. 65.
[b]Bank Markazi, *Annual Report and Balance Sheet 1975-76* (Teheran), p. 50. The series of figures for earlier years published in the Central Bank reports were higher than the figures that Tofiq presents, so the report data was used only where others were not available.

The increase in private capital formation from 1971 to 1975 was facilitated by the government's dramatically improved oil revenues. These revenues enabled the government to provide incentives to private sector investors in the form of supplemental financial capital for private projects and of joint public-private projects that were financially attractive. It is undoubtedly the case, too, that the prospects for future economic growth made investments look attractive.

Private investment might have been still higher if the government had shifted some of its military budget directly into infrastructural development projects that would improve the expected rates of return on investment. Those who think that military spending may contribute to economic growth often point to the possible civilian use of military infrastructure. Those kinds of spin-offs cannot, however, be assumed. Nor is there enough information available about the costs of providing civilian infrastructure through spin-offs from military investments.

As indicated in the previous chapter, the lack of internal transport was historically an impediment to the development of a national economy. During the 1970s, communications and transport investments in Iran were sizable. A high proportion of expenditures on communications were for the military (Table 4.3). Similar figures for transport are not available; certainly earlier, major transportation projects were military in origin. In one such case, during World War II, British engineers improved many kilometers of highways in Iran in order to transport munitions to the Soviet forces in the north.[12] The decisions about which highways to develop were made according to military criteria, not those of internal trade.

Similarly, the United States undertook to move the main railroad line during the war because it was not suitably located for military transport, and invested in approximately 180 locomotives and more than five thousand freight cars to add to the railroad's rolling stock. After the war, the railroad fell into disuse because it had no major role in civilian transport. Instead, the Iranian government channeled development funds into roads and highways. A number of the roads were primarily for military use, most clearly those that led north from the Gulf, parallel to the Iraqi border. That region, for the most part, is relatively sparsely populated. The roads' military value was that they provided access to an insecure border and to Kurdish and Luri tribal territories. From a security standpoint improving these roads was a logical step; however, the existence of additional kilometers of improved roads could not be counted as an increase in civilian economic infrastructure equal to road improvements that could have been made in other localities.

Iran's experience during the oil boom indicates that transport facilities and other infrastructure were inadequate to the needs of a rapidly developing economy. Some of the factors that impeded increases in domestic production were the presence of "bottlenecks" in the form of crowded ports and transport facilities, insufficient power that resulted in frequent outages, and, in the agricultural sector, inadequate storage, transport, and marketing facilities. As an alternative investment, military expenditures were competitive with other expenditures that might have stimulated continued economic growth.

DUALISM AND UNEVEN GROWTH

This conclusion is borne out, to a degree, by Iran's relatively poor record in accomplishments in the area of education and social welfare in contrast to other less industrialized countries. In 1975, when Iran's per capita income stood at an enviable $1,260 per year and when military spending was at a record high, Iran ranked *eighty-fifth* in literacy, *seventy-seventh* in life expectancy, and *one-hundred-and-sixth* in infant mortality.[13] Education and health received less than half the funding that the military did, using the most conservative estimates of military spending, a situation that was typical for the Middle East, but not for other Third World countries.

Related to the low physical quality of life for a majority of Iranians was the unevenness of growth throughout the economy. The disparity between urban and rural income was increasing, with a ratio of at least 5:1 in the mid-1970s. This process was officially explained as a "leading sector" phenomenon associated with early stages of industrialization which would disappear in the long run. Unofficially, however, many planners felt that this performance did not bode well for Iran's long-term economic growth.

The oil sector was the fastest growing in terms of earnings. In 1960 oil and gas accounted for ten percent of GDP; in 1974 the proportion was fifty-one percent. In actual production, mining and manufacturing increased during the 1960s by an annual rate of over 11 percent, but slowed after 1970 as oil production leveled off (Table 6.3). The rate of growth of the service sector, including government spending, was higher from 1970 to 1977 than it was from 1960 to 1970. The service sector characteristically includes a high proportion of underemployed persons; therefore, in some cases the growth of the services sector can be an indication of economic stagnation. However, Iran's services sector was not excessively large overall in comparison to most less industrialized countries.

Hidden in the overall economic growth, agriculture was not prospering. In theory, farm income could increase during industrialization, if the shift in demand for agricultural products were permitted to influence agricultural prices and production. But this did not happen. The reality of the agricultural sector was a low growth rate, poverty, and out-migration (see Chapter 8). Young people from farming communities could increase their incomes eightfold by moving to the city, where they could find construction work or even unskilled jobs.

In addition to uneven sectoral growth, a structural dualism existed, based on distinct markets and technology.[14] The modern sector, dominated by oil, was oriented toward foreign markets and used capital-intensive technologies. The labor-intensive traditional sector, which included the majority of the population, encompassed small-scale agricul-

TABLE 6.3

Sector Growth Rates
(average annual rates)

Sector	1960-1970	1970-1977
Agriculture	4.4	5.8
Industry	13.4	3.4
Services	10.0	16.8
GDP	11.3	7.8

Source: World Bank, *World Development Report,* 1979, p. 129. Industry includes construction and oil. The rates are calculated from constant price data.

ture and cottage industry. By the early 1970s the traditional economy still accounted for the largest share of employment. The low economic status of people working in this sector was indicated by the widening gap between urban and rural incomes.[15] By and large, the traditional sector was not stimulated by the oil because few of the inputs it used were produced domestically.

Military programs in the areas of weapons procurement, technology acquisition and, for the most part, construction were much the same as in the oil industry. Many of the programs' links were with the modern sector. Weapons procurement generally meant either imports or "enclave" arms production part (Chapter 4). Construction of the larger military installations was carried out by foreign contractors, such as Bechtel or Brown and Root, companies which worked on military construction all over the world. Personnel expenditures, which declined as a proportion of military expenditures, included increasingly large payments to highly skilled technical workers, many of whom were foreign (Chapter 9). Thus, given the regime's perception of what types of expenditures were required for military security, the contribution that they could make to economic growth in a dualistic economy was limited.

DEVELOPMENT FUNDING

Economic planners in less industrialized countries have recommended a variety of strategies to reduce dualism such as that just described because it is a constraint on growth. Most of the recommendations include government intervention as a mechanism to replace the market, which is not, by definition, equipped to respond to structural problems. Government intervention is accomplished through public investment, usually included in development budgets. Examining the relationship between development spending and military spending addresses this different dimension of the economic impact of military spending—whether there is any trade-off between military and development budgets.

Formal economic planning is relatively recent in Iran as elsewhere. It dates from the late 1940s, although in the 1930s government expenditures were divided into what were called "development" and "current" accounts. The first development plan was initiated in 1949. It was a project-oriented plan rather than a comprehensive and integrated one. The bureaucratic apparatus for preparing a comprehensive plan was not created until 1958 with the establishment of the Plan Organization (later, Plan and Budget Organization).

Over the years covered by the first five national development plans, development budgets and military spending evidenced an inverse relationship. Table 6.4 shows the ratio of development spending to military spending from the beginning of the First Plan until the end of the Fifth Plan in 1978. For four of the five planning periods, more funds were allocated to development than to military expenditures. The first planning period produced the lowest ratio. Two explanations for this finding are suggested: first, development planning was a new idea and it had few bureaucratic advocates; second, the timing was during the post-World War II military consolidation and overlapped with the beginning of the Mossadegh conflict.

The highest ratio of development to military spending occurred during the Third Plan period (1963-1967). Then, over the next two periods, the ratio declined. This progression represents the high point of the Plan Organization's political influence in the early 1960s, when the Third Plan was initiated and land reform and the "White Revolution" were introduced. The lowest ratio of development expenditures to military expenditures occurred during the First Plan. The relatively low ratio may

TABLE 6.4

Milex and Development Financing

| | National development plan | | | | |
	First	Second	Third	Fourth	Fifth
Ratio of development funds to Milex	.9	1.4	2.5	1.8	1.4

Sources: Jahangir Amuzegar and M.A. Fekrat, *Iran: Economic Development Under Dualistic Conditions* (Chicago: University of Chicago Press, 1971); Hossien Razavi and Firouz Vakil, *The Political Environment of Economic Planning in Iran 1971-1983* (Boulder, Col.: Westview Press, 1984), p. 71.

have resulted from the newness of development planning and the lack of bureaucratic support for the idea. In addition, the plan was constructed at a time when the Shah was particularly interested in building up the army as he consolidated his own power.

Following that period, the ministries began to reclaim some of the initiative from the Plan Organization *and* the military arms buildup began, with the shift toward weapons procurement as the focus of military budgets. Even though development and current expenditures were merged again in 1973, development planners were less involved in budget decisions as the buildup gained momentum (see Chapter 3). And, as seen in the last chapter, development expenditures were singled out as a target for cuts in 1977, when inflation and government overspending were finally addressed.

Once again, official budget statistics can be misleading. It is known that some military expenditures were included in the development budgets. The bias brought into the analysis through the changing and uncertain reporting techniques is almost certainly a repeated bias in the direction of exaggerating actual development expenditures. In the 1940s, according to Fekrat and Amuzegar,[16] development expenditures included arms and munitions imports. During the Fifth Plan, one-third of the development budget represented funding for specific military projects, some of which have been described in other chapters.* Thus, the ratio for the Fifth Plan was derived by dividing two-thirds of Fifth Plan expenditures by official national defense figures for the five-year period through 1977.

---

*It is likely that other governments bring military projects under the umbrella of development. In 1984 the Malaysian government was using the same procedure when budgeting the military. Military expenditures amounted to about one-third of Malaysia's total development budget.

POLITICAL PERSPECTIVES

One of the most difficult questions about "guns-or-butter" decisions is why they are made in one direction rather than another. There is no simple answer to this question. Bureaucratic politics, personal influence, and external political pressures all played a role in determining how military spending decisions were made. Ideological commitments to particular models of development also were part of the context of resource allocation.

Looking at the record of government investments in the economy, Looney concluded that the Shah was pursuing the same development goal that his father had—that of a modern industrial society.[17] Investments in small-scale agriculture, in traditional cottage industries and, it could be added, in social investments that did not directly contribute to industrialization and technological advance were neglected relative to these two areas.

Decisions about the government's economic investments resembled military spending decisions in one or two important respects. First, physical capital was given exceptional importance. In earlier chapters we characterized the Shah's military security policies as being increasingly "hardware focused" as opposed to fundamentally political. The economic equivalent was the emphasis on (imported) intermediate and capital goods rather than looking at the functioning of the entire economy and integrating new capital and technology into the productive activity that already existed.

Leonard Binder described the Shah's approach to development policy as "future shock . . . considered virtuous."[18] One interpretation of why he adopted this kind of approach to development and security policy is that it served to protect the Shah from the political process. Military hardware and industrial technology could be purchased without negotiating with anyone within Iran, even though broader support would eventually be necessary to the success of these programs. In the case of the government's investment decisions, the choices that were made were not the product of political accommodation to private sector interests, nor did they take account of the interests of the still-dominant traditional sector, especially from the time of the Fourth Plan. In the case of military security, the policies did not acknowledge the ideas of those who had a more political view of security and believed that a more dynamic political process would contribute to that goal.

Like his father, Mohammad Reza Shah initially built his regime around the army and, unlike his father, on U.S. support for the army (see Chapter 2). To both, the clergy and the bazaar were archaic institutions. The two men's attitudes helped to polarize Iranian politics. Opposition groups active after World War II—Islamic, leftist, and the National Front—shared the view that military spending was directly related to U.S. support for the Shah rather than to national security interests.

SUMMARY

Iran's aggregate economic growth rates from 1950 to 1980 were high in comparison to other less industrialized countries and at least average for oil-producing countries. Military spending did not preclude growth as measured by the concurrent rate of growth in Iran's GDP. Under the assumption that the impact of military spending on economic growth is felt over a period of years, a time factor was introduced. This did suggest that there might have been a correspondence between high rates of growth in military spending and lower subsequent economic growth rates. Nevertheless, private capital formation did increase somewhat through 1977 as a proportion of the GNP.

The growth that did occur was not evenly distributed. The agricultural sector experienced the lowest growth rate, and rural incomes were low. The Iranian government's record in providing health and education to its population was not good compared to countries that were much poorer. In this context, the Shah's willingness to allow development budgets to shrink relative to military expenditures was particularly costly for the long-term prospects for growth.

The economy's structural dualism both helped to account for the uneven growth and inequality that existed and stood in the way of its amelioration through military spending, when military spending became oriented toward advanced-technology hardware. This orientation was compatible with the Shah's views on development and with his distaste for politics, but it did not contribute to military-led economic growth.

NOTES

1. Manoucher Parvin, "Military Expenditure in Iran: A Forgotten Question," *Iranian Studies* 1 (Autumn 1968): 149-154.

2. Theodore H. Moran, "Iranian Defense Expenditures and the Social Crisis," *International Security* 3, 3 (Winter 1978/1979): 178-192; Stephanie Neuman, "Security, Military Expenditures, and Socio-economic Development: Reflections on Iran," *Orbis* 22, 3 (Fall 1978): 569 Table 6.594.

3. Nicole Ball, *Security and Economy in the Third World: The Role of Security Expenditure in the Development Process* (Princeton: Princeton University Press, 1989), p. 47.

4. Robert Looney and P.C. Frederiksen, "Defense Expenditures and Post-Revolutionary Iranian Economic Growth," *Armed Forces and Society* 9, 4 (Summer 1983): 634-646.

5. Wassily Leontief and Faye Duchin, *Military Spending: Facts and Figures, Worldwide Implications and Future Outlook* (New York: Oxford University Press, 1983).

6. Charles Issawi, "The Iranian Economy 1925-1975: Fifty Years of Economic Development," in George Lenczowski, ed., *Iran Under the Pahlavis* (Stanford, Calif.: Hoover Institution Press, 1978), p. 162.

7. World Bank, *World Development Report 1979* (New York: Oxford University Press, 1979), p. 129.

8. Emile Benoit, *Defense and Economic Growth in Developing Countries* (Lexington, Mass.: Lexington Books, 1973), p. 72.

9. Ali E. Dessouki and Abdel al-Labban, "Arms Race, Defense Expenditures, and Development: The Egyptian Case 1952-1973," *Journal of South Asian and Middle Eastern Studies* 4, 3 (Spring 1981): 65-71.

10. Hossein Askari and Vittorio Gorbo, "Economic Implications of Military Expenditures in the Middle East," *Journal of Peace Research* 2 (1974): 341-343.

11. For a discussion of the general question of alternative investments, see Nicole Ball, "Defense Expenditures and Economic Growth: A Comment," *Armed Forces and Society* 11, 2 (Winter 1985): 291-297.

12. Raj Narain Gupta, *Iran: An Economic Study* (New Delhi: Indian Institute of International Affairs, 1947).

13. Ruth L. Sivard, *World Military and Social Expenditures* (Leesburg, Va.: World Priorities, 1979), Table 3.

14. Jahangir Amuzegar and M. Ali Fekrat, *Iran: Economic Development Under Dualistic Conditions* (Chicago: University of Chicago Press, 1971).

15. Firouz Vakil, "Iran's Basic Macroeconomic Problems: A Twenty-Year Horizon," in Jane W. Jacqz, ed., *Iran: Past, Present and Future* (New York: Aspen Institute for Humanistic Studies, 1976), p. 90.

16. Amuzegar and Fekrat, *Iran*, p. 21.

17. Robert E. Looney, *Economic Origins of the Iranian Revolution* (Elmsford, N.Y.: Pergamon Press, 1982), p. 10.

18. Leonard Binder, "Iran," *The Political Economy of the Middle East 1973-78: A Compendium of Papers*, Submitted to the Joint Economic Committee, Congress of the United States (Washington, D.C.: U.S. Government Printing Office, 1980), p. 163.

SEVEN

The Industrial Sector

Iran's industrial sector grew rapidly from 1960 to 1980. Existing consumer goods industries, established in the 1930s, were expanded. Iran's oil resources made it possible for the government to broaden the scope of investment into more capital-intensive, advanced-technology industries. A beginning was made in the domestic production of consumer, intermediate, and capital goods, as well as in metal and mineral processing. Many, but not all, of these industries were financed and managed by the state.

The modernization of Iran's industrial sector began at a time when the economy was still basically agricultural, creating the dualism described in the previous chapter. The modern industries introduced during the 1960s and 1970s were superimposed on a manufacturing sector that consisted predominantly of small-scale workshops, which accounted for as much as eighty percent of manufacturing employment.[1]

To attempt to build an industrial economy from such a base, over a short period of time, was an ambitious goal. The disparity between the industrial development policies designed to achieve this goal and the economic and social realities helped to disrupt the tenuous accommodations among social groups that had permitted the monarchy to survive through earlier generations.[2] Many critics of government policy have focused their explanations of the revolution specifically on this failure to invest in human resources and economic infrastructure to the extent required for a smooth transition to an industrialized economy.[3]

Apart from the impact of industrialization on political stability is the question of whether the military programs initiated by the Shah contributed to or detracted from the process of industrialization in Iran. This chapter looks at industrial growth rates and the government's industrial development plans. Historians see industrialization and military development as closely linked in the experience of other countries; many contemporary leaders also see them as compatible.

TRENDS IN INDUSTRIAL PRODUCTION

In general, industrialization did proceed rapidly, encouraged by the regime's determination to build an economic foundation for Iran's growing military power. Industrial growth rates in Iran increased steadily for at least two decades before the revolution (Table 7.1). From 1963 to 1972, the last year of the Fourth National Development Plan, the number of large industrial establishments rose from several hundred to about six thousand. Value added in industry grew at an average annual rate of 16.4 percent during the Third Plan (1963-1967); 13.7 percent during the Fourth Plan (1968-1972); and at an estimated 24 percent during the Fifth Plan (1973-1978).[4] According to official statistics, the rate of industrial growth increased from 5 percent in 1962 to over 20 percent in 1974.[5] Consequently, from 1959 to 1974 the share of manufacturing and mining in nonoil GNP had risen from 19 to 29 percent.

The industrial sector experienced a period of growth in the late 1950s, but it was largely limited to traditional industries. During the 1960s a variety of new industries were established, including steel and aluminum, petrochemicals, machine tools, tractors and automobiles, electronics, pulp and paper, and a variety of consumer goods. By 1976 these industries accounted for nearly thirty-five percent of total nonoil exports.[6] Investment in machinery and equipment for the industrial and mining sector grew at an annual rate of fourteen percent during the 1960s and early 1970s.[7] Government investment emphasized heavy industry. Steel and aluminum production increased ninety-four percent per year from 1965 to 1974.[8]

There is no doubt that industrial and military modernization occurred simultaneously. The statistics show that the highest growth rate in industrial value added occurred at the time of the highest growth rate in military spending. And, rates of growth in value added were consistently high throughout the period of military spending increases. The record from 1962 until 1975 indeed suggests that military spending contributed to industrialization.

TABLE 7.1

Industrial Value Added/Military Expenditures

Year	Value added[a] (billion rials)	Ratio to GNP	Years	Average annual growth	
				Value added	National defense[b]
1959	63.5	15.7			
1960	67.8	16.1			
1961	72.9	16.8	1962-	18.4	25.3
1962	79.0	17.4	67		
1963	89.2	18.6			
1964	93.8	17.9			
1965	111.8	19.1			
1966	123.3	19.2			
1967	143.6	20.0			
1968	159.3	20.0	1968-	13.7	35.1
1969	172.2	19.9	72		
1970	188.3	19.7			
1971	215.4	20.4			
1972	246.5	20.1			
1973	286.6	15.8	1973-	24.4	53.8
1974	351.1	13.8	75		
1975	426.2	16.4			

Source: Firouz Vakil, "A Development Strategy for Iran: The Role of the Public Sector" (Teheran: Plan and Budget Organization, Planometrics and General Economy Bureau, September 1976), mimeo, p. 9. Vakil's figures for value added are at variance with other published statistics; they may, in fact, be current prices. They are the only published series that extends to 1975. The rates of growth specified by the various series are comparable. National defense figures are from official government budgets.
[a]Constant 1972 prices.
[b]Constant 1975 prices.

The overlap at the policy level between state-initiated civilian and military industrialization is reflected in military industrial accounting, as described in Chapter 4. The industries experiencing the highest rates of growth during the Fourth Plan, which marked the beginning of the Shah's accelerated weapons procurement programs, were those producing intermediate and capital goods, which included military goods (Table 7.2) (discussed more below). As long as the investment in and production of military industries are not entirely separated from civilian industries, aggregate investment and production statistics are not a reliable basis for determining whether military expenditures promote or deter industrialization.

Another problem with the industrial statistics is that those for the Fifth Plan period include only two years. They do not reflect what hap-

TABLE 7.2

Real Growth Rates of Specific Industries
(1967=100)

Industry	1968-1972	1967-1968
Food	7.0	1.1
Beverages	11.0	9.7
Textiles, rugs	10.3	5.4
Clothing and materials	7.2	11.6
Wood and furniture	9.2	1.6
Paper and cardboard	12.5	1.9
Hides and leather	-1.0	20.4[a]
Tires	13.3	
Chemicals	41.7	35.6
Nonmetal construction materials	11.9	
Metallurgical industries	19.2	22.4
Metal products	16.1	
Nonelectrical machinery	5.9	69.3[b]
Electrical machinery	23.5	
Transportation vehicles	31.5	75.9
Miscellaneous	23.5	
General index	14.2	15.2

Sources: For 1968-1972: Bank Markazi Iran, *Annual Report and Balance Sheet,* 1351 (1972), 1967=100; for 1967-1968: p. 164, 1964=100.
[a] For 1967-1968, this category includes rubber and leather products.
[b] For 1967-1968, this category includes machinery and road vehicles.

pened to industry during the period of economic instability that set in after 1975. There were other indications that future industrial growth might not be as high as during the early 1970s. The ratio of investment in machinery to that in construction fell between 1972 and 1977 from .65 to .54.[9]

Second, the ratio of industrial value added to GNP was not increasing over time. And, third, the value-added data refer to total value added by industrial goods finished in Iran. Domestic value added was much lower. The industries established under the Fourth Plan began at a later stage of production; the intention was to work backward to self-sufficiency. One estimate of domestic value added was one-third of the total.[10]

Another economist concluded that domestic value added by industrial goods produced in Iran would be negative if their prices were calculated on the basis of world market prices; that is, their prices were inflated by government protection policies.[11] These estimates are of value added in the industrial sector as a whole. They are corroborated by data, included below, showing the high import requirements of domestic industries.

STATE PLANNING AND INDUSTRIAL GROWTH

The national industrial development plans had a considerable influence on the direction of industrialization, given that Iran was at such an early stage in that process. The financial resources were available to the government to undertake industrial investments and in conjunction with private industry. Planning also involved the private sector through regulations concerning profits, location, equity, and other matters. Therefore, a review of the plans helps to explain the statistics presented in the previous section.

The Third Plan (1963-1967). The period during which the Third Plan was in effect was one in which economic planning and social change were beginning in earnest. Land redistribution was initiated in 1962; subsequent reforms were introduced as the White Revolution. It also was a period of balanced growth and relatively modest military ambitions. Military spending was relatively low in comparison to development spending (see Table 6.3 in the previous chapter), although it was toward the end of the plan that military spending began its rapid growth. The Plan Organization had authority over all development funds, irrespective of which ministry would implement the projects. These were the years during which military and civilian officials consulted on budgetary matters, and, in the course of their meetings, reviewed the military budget in the larger context of government spending.[12]

Beginning with the Third Plan in 1963, the national development plans were constructed around specific growth strategies and emphasized investments in certain industries more than others. The decisions that were made for the Third Plan regarding industrial investments reflected the political atmosphere at that time. With $350 million in investments, industry and mining received eleven percent of the funds spent through the plan. Unlike the subsequent plans, this one distributed the industrial investments among projects in both the traditional and modern industrial sectors (Table 7.3). The sums invested in food processing and textiles were nearly as large as those invested in chemicals and metals. Steel and petrochemical projects were planned, but did not get under way to any significant extent.

The Fourth Plan (1968-1972). With the beginning of the Fourth Plan, the government's financial resources had increased, as had its military ambitions. Government investments in traditional industries dwindled and a substantial shift was initiated from consumer goods to intermediate and capital goods. Industry and mining received a much larger twenty-one percent of total Fourth Plan funds. In real terms, investment in industrial and mining equipment grew by fourteen percent. Credits for mechanical, electrical, and transport industries increased fivefold. Several metallurgical, machine-tool, and aluminum-smelting projects were begun.

Toward the end of the Fourth Plan the first military aircraft and electronics facilities were established, as described in Chapter 4. These military projects were perceived as precursors to civilian aircraft and electronics industries. According to one of the central figures in Iran's military industries, the strategy of beginning with military production was an appropriate one, and he added that Iran's electronics industry "would not have gotten off the ground were it not for the military."[13] General Katorijan, quoted earlier, concurred with this conclusion. The assumption was widely held among supporters of military-led industrialization that private sector investors were not likely to take the initiative in electronics, or other high-technology industries, without being "shown the way" by the military.

Although there was evidence to support this assumption, it would be a more credible explanation of government policy if the private sector had been invited to participate in military projects to the extent that it could have been (Chapter 4). It also begs the question of whether investments in those sectors were warranted by the market for those goods and whether other industries offered potentially more appropriate and profitable alternatives at that stage of industrialization. Finally, the military projects relied on imports.

With so many military and civilian projects under way, the demand for intermediate goods rose far more rapidly than domestic supply. Three-quarters of the metallurgical and metal-working equipment sold in Iran was imported. Domestic production of intermediate goods met slightly more than one percent of demand for the Fourth Plan; about sixty

TABLE 7.3

State Investment in Industry: Development Credits

Industry	3rd Plan (1963-1967) %	4th Plan (1968-1972) %	5th Plan[a] (1973-1978) %
Food processing and tobacco	35.7	5.4	4.4
Metal smelting (base metals, steel)	22.6	50.9	29.3
Mechanical, electrical, transportation (incl. "machinery" in 4th and "rubber" in 3rd)	2.7	10.1	17.7
Chemicals and petrochemicals	22.6	24.1	21.6
Nonmetallic minerals	—	—	—
Other industries (incl. "rural," 4th and 5th; "textile," 3rd)	12.7	.8	1.5
Training and research		.9	2.9
Exploration of mines		1.2	—
Assistance to private sector investors[b]		6.8	10.3
Cellulose, printing			7.7
General services[c]			3.6
Recurrent projects			1.0
Building	3.2		
Soap	.5		
Total	100.0	100.1	100.0

Sources: *Third Plan*, pp. 94-95; *Fourth Plan*, p. 129; *Fifth Plan*, p. 58.
[a]These figures are from the original Fifth Plan, before it was revised to take into account increased oil revenues.
[b]Third Plan allocations to the private sector were not separated from the public sector.
[c]Includes expenses of the Military Industries Organization, but the specific expenses were not recorded.

percent of Iran's import bill in the 1970s was for the purchase of intermediate and capital goods. The Military Industries Organization was the
largest single purchaser of machine tools, exceeding even the State Industrial Development and Reconstruction Organization. In this respect the
military projects were in direct competition with civilian industries, private sector and state owned.

One of the objectives the regime hoped to accomplish as new industries were established was to reduce Teheran's dominance as an industrial center. This was seen as desirable from the standpoint of military objectives and of balanced development. Approximately sixty
percent of Iran's entire industrial production occurred in Teheran or the
Central Province.[14] Teheran attracted industries because it was the center
of government and the infrastructure was there. In addition, industrial
managers wanted to be near government offices with which they needed
to carry out transactions associated with government financing and regulations; the lack of communications and transportation made it difficult
to accomplish this from other parts of the country.

One means by which industrial decentralization was to be accomplished was to give preferential financing to new industries that were
willing to locate in one of four provincial cities—Tabriz, Ahwaz, Arak, or
Esfahan—rather than Teheran. Almost half of all loans were made to industries located in the provinces. The government also began to decen-
tralize state-owned industries. Oil shipping and refining facilities were
moved south along the Gulf coast away from Iraq. New military plants
were located in several centers, of which Esfahan was to be the most important.

The Fifth Plan (1973-1978). Planners continued to attempt to de-
centralize economic growth by means of a regional development program introduced in the Fifth Plan. The program encouraged provincial
officials to become involved in the planning process. However, the program had a minuscule budget ($270 million) in contrast to the sums being
spent for military and infrastructure projects. As oil revenues leveled off
in the mid-1970s, a number of the regional development projects were actually canceled or remained unfinished. The director of regional planning argued that as a result of its inadequate funding, the government's
decisions about where military and infra-structure projects would be located had a much greater impact on regional development than did the
Fifth Plan program itself.

Overall, the Fifth Plan represented a shift in priorities away from industrialization and toward infrastructure projects, including electrical power, communications, and transport. In the original Fifth Plan, which was drawn up before the oil price rise of 1973-1974, 12.1 percent of the development budget was allocated to industry and mining, with industry to receive 194.5 billion rials, or approximately $3 billion. When the plan was revised to reflect Iran's improved financial situation, fixed investment in industry and mining amounted to 18 percent of the budget, or 339 billion rials.[15]

Appropriations for industry from the development budget under the revised plan did not keep pace with those of other sectors of the economy.[16] If the original industrial allocations had been increased proportionately with the increase in revenues (i.e., quadrupled), industry's share of the revised plan would have been approximately 778 billion rials. Nor was the amount of money invested in industry even close to the amounts expended on the military. For 1977, for example, the official (and, thus, low) estimate of military spending was $8.6 billion. This sum was almost as large as *total* government investment in industry for the entire Fifth Plan.

The Fifth Plan stated several objectives for industrial development. One was to capitalize on Iran's relative advantage in power-intensive industries and petrochemicals. A second was to pursue an export-promotion policy in place of the import-substitution emphasis of previous plans. Military spending was connected to these two objectives in several ways. Iran's import bills had been rising rapidly and military spending contributed to that increase. The gap between nonoil export earnings and the value of imports was as high as $19 billion in the mid-1970s. Under liberal assumptions about domestic production for import substitution and potential exports by the agriculture and service sector, industrial exports would need to increase by sixty times over their 1976 levels in order to meet the need for foreign exchange in 1991.[17]

Another link between military spending and industrial growth was the decision about what industries to invest in; industrial development funds were going directly into military industries. Most public investment in mechanical industries was military, as was a third of chemical and petrochemical investment (Table 7.4). Chemical and petrochemical industries were growing rapidly, with investments from the government, foreign corporations and, to a lesser extent, private domestic investors.

TABLE 7.4

Military Industry in the Fifth Plan and 1977 Budget
(in billions of rials)

Industry	Fifth Plan[a]	1977 budget
Automotive	9.16	7.4
military	1.16	1.2
civilian	8.	6.2
Chemical and petrochemical	45.	2.6
military	14.	2.6
civilian	31.	insignificant
Mechanical	28.7	6.9
military	22.2	4.2
civilian	6.5	2.7
Electronics		1.8
military		1.8
civilian		insignificant
Total industry	199.6	115.7
military	37.4	9.8
civilian	162.2	105.9

Sources: Fifth Plan, p. 60; *Kayhan,* March 12, 1977.
[a]Fifth Plan figures refer to projected investments in public sector industrial projects for the original, unrevised plan.

In a few cases, however, such as the establishment of a nuclear power industry, the objectives did not coincide. Iran had both uranium deposits and a growing demand for electrical power. But it did not have the industrial capacity to make efficient use of nuclear generating plants, given that the initial costs of importing turnkey power plants were enormous. The first contracts undertaken for reactors and technical support amounted to almost ten percent of Iran's total import bill. The most likely explanation for the sizable investment in nuclear plants—which the Islamic regime has continued—was that the Shah wanted to keep Iran's nuclear option open.

INDUSTRIAL FINANCE

Iran's industrial sector was a mixed one in terms of public/private investment and ownership. Some enterprises were solely state owned, others were financed jointly, and still others were totally private. Although government policy was to promote a mixed economy, the share of private investment in total industrial investment declined, partly due to the state's growing oil revenues. In 1960 private investment represented 71.7 percent of the total; in 1972 it represented 45.6 percent.[18]

The Fifth Plan projected an increase in private investment to two-thirds of the total. Although figures for actual private investment in industry are not available for that period, it is likely that the proportion did not increase to that level and may have declined. The ratio of private to public investment for the economy as a whole went from 1.53 in 1963, to 1.00 in 1972, to .74 in 1977.

Three-fourths of all private investment was mobilized through equity and/or loan arrangements with state development banks (Table 7.5), the largest of which was the Industrial and Mining Development Bank of Iran. Funding for the bank's projects came from foreign investors (sixty-seven percent) and from the Iranian government (thirty-three percent). The IMBDI's lending policies gave preference to relatively large-scale enterprises, with $1 million being the average loan.[19]

In addition to its direct investments, other government policies also influenced the direction of industrial development in the private sector toward relatively large-scale, capital-intensive production. As described earlier, this was accomplished by providing financial incentives to particular investors in the form of offering joint financing, granting licenses, water and power subsidies, tax incentives, and import permits. Capital goods could be imported duty-free. The Ministry of Economy promoted large-scale manufacturing establishments through its licensing policies.

The government tried to encourage foreign investment, but it was not very successful. Private foreign investment did not amount to more than six percent of the total. Many of the large-scale projects were in chemical and petrochemical industries. The National Petrochemical Corporation was involved in several joint ventures with foreign corporations, including Amoco International, Allied Chemical, and Mitsui, as well as having plants of its own. These ventures were focused on producing for the export market. The government was participating in a joint venture with B.F. Goodrich to produce PVCs, caustics, and detergent for domestic use.

TABLE 7.5

Sources of Investment in Industry: 1962-1972
(millions of rials)

Source	Amount	Percentage
Total public	137,000	38.3
Total private	220,245	61.7
Mobilized by dev. banks[a]	120,540	54.7
Nonbank sources	45,213	20.5
Foreign private	3,500	6.0

Source: Firouz Sadigh, *Impact of Government Policies on the Structure and Growth of Iranian Industry 1960-1972* (Faculty of Economics, University of London, 1975), p. 69.
[a]Industrial Mining and Development Bank, 73.8%; Industrial Credit Bank, 21.6%; Bank Omran, 4.6%.

In 1955 the parliament, which was controlled by the Shah, passed a Law for the Attraction and Promotion of Foreign Investment, which was intended to reassure potential investors that the days in which the nationalization of oil was possible were over. The law allowed foreign investors to repatriate their profits. But a combination of politics and the lack of potential profits led a representative for a Japanese firm to declare "we are offered the 'dregs' of the international market" when told that his government had "assigned" Iran to them.[20] In 1975, when the Shah announced a ceiling on foreign ownership of forty-nine percent of joint corporations, foreign investors were further discouraged.

INDUSTRIAL PROJECTIONS

Iranian government economists made a series of projections concerning the level of investments that would be required to maintain and/or improve growth rates in each sector of the economy over the period of the Sixth Plan (which was never implemented).[21] Comparing these projections with military spending and with past levels of investment is another way of looking at the opportunity costs of military spending and how they might have come into play had more years elapsed between the arms buildup and the revolution.

Given these projections, it is reasonable to state that attaining the growth rates suggested by the Plan and Budget Organization would have required changing the ratio between military and civilian industrial investments. According to the estimates, an annual investment of $3 billion would have been required to maintain an industrial growth rate of 12.8 percent, an increase of one-third over the 1978 level. In terms of military expenditures, the amount of increase in industrial investment required to attain Sixth Plan objectives would be equivalent to only ten percent of military spending during the Fifth Plan. However, the spending decisions that were made during the Fifth Plan gave no indication that the industrial sector would receive a larger share of investment in the future if the funds had to be taken from the military sector. Although theoretically funds could have been shifted to industry from other sectors besides the military, in actuality the overall development budget was minimal.

SUMMARY

Iran's industrial sector in the late 1970s was very different from that of 1960 and earlier. Modern industries had been established and were producing a variety of goods for the domestic market and for export. Overall, official figures showing value added in industry indicated that industrialization was proceeding at a rapid rate compared to other Third World countries, although in later years the ratio of industrial value added to GNP did begin to decline slightly. Industry, like the military, was becoming more capital intensive and this kept *domestic* value added low. And, because of the need for foreign exchange, industrial development policy became increasingly export oriented.

In these respects, state-run industrial development was generally compatible with military policy. In fact, in some areas they overlapped directly. A substantial portion of state development funds went to electrical, chemical, and mechanical industries producing military goods. The overlap between investments in industry and in the military sector presents the most troublesome issue in assessing the military's contribution to industrialization. The portion of military expenditures that is allocated to industrial goods and services is most commonly included in overall industrial statistics. However, the industrial growth that they imply does not necessarily stimulate civilian or long-term industrial growth.

Although the high proportion of imports in industrial inputs does not necessarily indicate the presence of restraints on long-term industrial growth, it does underline the uncertainty that accompanies planned industrialization. An industrialization process that involves importing very specific advanced technologies is different from the lengthier process which the first countries to industrialize went through in introducing largely indigenous technologies as the market rendered them profitable. For Iran during the 1970s, there were few signs that military expenditures were stimulating the industrial sector to produce intermediate and capital goods. Subsequent industrial performance is not a good indication of the results of these policies either, because the revolution and the war with Iraq created a unique situation.

What we know about Iran's brief experience with industrialization during a period of military modernization raises as many questions as it answers. The process of industrialization was under way, but it is not known how fast it might have proceeded if industrial development funds had been invested in the production of goods for domestic consumption rather than weapons, or if industries could have acquired foreign exchange more cheaply. Nor is it known whether or not industry would have grown more rapidly if state development plans had not emphasized large-scale, capital-intensive industry—a phenomenon that was partially connected to the concept of Iran as a significant military-industrial power.

NOTES

1. Hassan Hakimian, "Iran: Dependency and Industrialization," *Bulletin* 12, 1 (1980): 24.

2. Robert E. Looney, *Economic Origins of the Iranian Revolution* (Elmsford N.Y.: Pergamon Press, 1982), p. 18.

3. See, e.g., Norris S. Hetherington, "Industrialization and Revolution in Iran: Forced Progress or Unmet Expectation?" *Middle East Journal* 36, 3 (Summer 1982): 362-373.

4. Firouz Vakil, "A Development Strategy for Iran: The Role of the Public Sector" (Iran, Plan and Budget Organization, Planometrics and General Economy Bureau, September 1976), mimeo, p. 9. As indicated in the note to Table 7.1, there is considerable variation in the published statistics showing value added in industry. For another set, see Charles Issawi, "The Iranian Economy 1925-1975: Fifty Years of Economic Development," in George Lenczowski, ed., *Iran Under the Pahlavis* (Stanford, Calif.: Hoover Institution Press, 1978), p. 152.

5. F. Najmabadi, "Strategies of Industrial Development in Iran," in Jane W. Jacqz, ed., *Iran: Past, Present and Future* (New York: Aspen Institute for Humanistic Studies, 1976), p. 106.

6. Issawi, "The Iranian Economy," p. 152.

7. Iran, Bank Markazi, *Annual Report and Balance Sheet 1972*, p. 199.

8. Issawi, "The Iranian Economy," p. 152.

9. Looney, *Economic Origins*, p. 67.

10. Hakimian, "Iran," p. 25.

11. Firouz Sadigh, *Impact of Government Policies on the Structure and Growth of Iranian Industry 1960-1972* (Faculty of Economics, University of London, 1975), p. 15.

12. This history is based on interviews with people who regularly attended the meetings.

13. Personal interview.

14. Harold Mehner, "Development and Planning in Iran After World War II," in Lenczowski, *Iran Under the Pahlavis*, p. 179.

15. Robert Graham, *The Illusion of Power* (New York: St. Martin's Press, 1978), p. 81.

16. Najmabadi, "Strategies of Industrial Development," p. 106.

17. Iran, Plan and Budget Organization, *Sixth Plan Policy Questions* (Planning Division, Planometrics and General Economy Bureau, June 1976).

18. Wilfried Korby, *Probleme der Industriallen Entwicklung und Konzentration in Iran*, Beihafte zum Tubinger Atlas des Vorderen Orients 13, 20 (Wiesbaden: Dr. Ludwig Reichert Verlag, 1977), p. 67.

19. Ibid., p. 93.

20. AMPO (Tokyo).

21. Iran, Plan and Budget Organization, *Sixth Plan Policy Questions*.

EIGHT

Agriculture

As the slowest-growing sector in Iran's economy, agricultural development is an important question in this discussion of military spending. We need to look at the whole range of factors that affected agricultural production in order to put military spending into perspective: the country's high population-growth rates, the natural limitations of Iran's farmland, and the increasing intervention of the government in agriculture.

Iran's geography (and, therefore, its agricultural potential) varies widely from one part of the country to another. Most of the land is either marginal or unusable for farming. Half of the country's total area is arid or semiarid with sparse vegetation. Rainfed farming is limited to the northern provinces of Khorrasan, Gilan, Mazandaran, and Azerbaijan. Rural incomes and population density are correspondingly higher in the north. Farmers in Azerbaijan earned more than $550 a year in the mid-1970s, in contrast to $8 a year for farmers in southeastern Baluchistan. Most of the crops are food crops. Wheat and barley account for forty-five percent of total agricultural production, followed by rice, cotton, and tobacco.

Agricultural production also was affected by politics. Iran's limited agricultural potential and its regional variations have made it particularly difficult to work out a coherent national agricultural policy. Beginning with Reza Shah, the policy was dominated by the extension of state control over farmlands, which was accomplished through increasing state ownership and through the process of mechanizing farms through government agencies. In 1962 a major land redistribution program was initiated; in subsequent years the program was revised several times and new experiments in agricultural organization were tried.

117

By the 1970s Iran was financially able to supplement its own food production with imports. A World Bank survey of Iranian agriculture recommended that Iran continue to import food as a matter of policy because the agricultural sector did not have a comparative advantage relative to the food-exporting countries.[1] This outlook may help to explain why agriculture was not a priority in development plans, particularly the Fourth and Fifth plans. There were other issues, as well, that came into play in government policy which we will look at from the political perspective of military security and military spending.

AGRICULTURAL PRODUCTION

The performance of the agricultural sector during the last two decades of the monarchy was mixed. According to one set of figures, total agricultural production increased during most of those years (Table 8.1). With the country's rapid population growth, the per capita agricultural growth was much less. In 1978 the *average* daily caloric consumption was 3,139, considerably higher than the 2,300 minimum. However, food was distributed unevenly and several detailed surveys showed that malnutrition was manifest in diseases like marasma, kwashiorkor, anemia, and rickets.[2]

The World Bank's 1974 report noted that official statistics tended to overestimate production. Other estimates for agricultural growth in the 1970s have described growth rates as low as negative four percent, although in specific years, like 1975, production could be much higher. As far as the rest of the economy was concerned, agriculture definitely was becoming a less important part of the economy. Its contribution to the GNP fell from twenty-nine percent in 1960 to ten percent in 1977.[3]

Agriculture continued to be significant in terms of employment, however. In 1978 forty percent of all employed persons in Iran were still working in agriculture. Agricultural production was not very efficient. Weinbaum constructed an index to measure efficiency by using the ratio of the sector's share in GDP to its share in employment. Using this index, he concluded that Iran was one of the least efficient agricultural producers in the Middle East, with a ratio that fell from .54 in 1960 to .22 in 1978.[4] Productivity per acre also was relatively low, particularly on farms using traditional technologies.[5] The yields that Iranian farmers achieved were

TABLE 8.1

Indices of Agricultural Production
(1952-1954 = 100)

Years	Total production	Per capita production
1935-39	85	118
1957-58	117	106
1959-60	123	106
1974-75	146	105
1975-76	167	116

Sources: Merip 43 (1976) p. 6, for figures through 1960; Michael Kurtzig, "U.S. Farm Sales to Iran Have Headed Downward," *Foreign Agriculture* 14, 21 (May 24, 1976): 3, for 1974 and 1975, with 1961-1965 as base years.

less than those of most other Middle Eastern countries. For example, wheat production was 340 kilos per hectare below the regional average.

In the 1970s the effective demand for food exceeded domestic production, and food imports grew accordingly. In the six years from 1972 to 1978, the proportion of imports in total food consumption rose from seven percent to thirty or forty percent. These imports cost at least $2 billion in 1978. Most of the imports came from the United States, the U.S. Department of Agriculture having promoted the exchanges through credits during earlier years.

The rest of the economy experienced other kinds of problems as a result of the slow growth rates in agriculture. Rural poverty contributed to urban migration rates of more than five percent annually. Many remained despite the limited opportunities for work. A household survey undertaken in 1970 concluded that 16 percent of the labor force in agriculture was working less than 28 hours a week and another 22 percent of the labor force was working less than 42 hours a week.[6]

FINANCING AGRICULTURAL DEVELOPMENT

Part of the explanation for low growth was, and is, land quality. Iran's agricultural potential has been described as low-to-moderate in comparison with the region as a whole.[7] Another reason was that government policy, although interventionist, did not provide adequate financing for the programs that it initiated. A former official in the Shah's government said that, in retrospect, "if we had done one thing differently, it would have been to strike a balance between industry and agriculture."

The proportion of development funds allocated to agriculture did decline abruptly from 22.5 percent of the Third Plan budget to 13.5 percent of the Fourth (Table 8.2). During the Fifth Plan the share increased to eighteen percent; but this sum included food subsidies, which amounted to approximately *half* of the total investment in agriculture.[8] Without the food subsidies, agriculture's share of development expenditures was approximately seven percent.

By the Fourth Plan, the government began to provide significant levels of financing to agribusiness, in particular those with foreign participation. Allocations made to agribusiness rose in the Fifth Plan (Table 8.3). In 1975 nearly two-thirds of the Agriculture Development Bank's subsidized low interest rate loans went to agribusiness ($424 million of a total of $696 million). A government loan to a consortium composed of the Agricultural Development Machinery Organization, the Industrial Mining and Development Bank, and Massey-Ferguson paid for eighty percent of the consortium's investment costs. The loan carried an interest rate of six percent at a time when private farm loans were carrying interest rates as high as fifty percent.

Despite government financing for agribusiness, in the course of the Fourth Plan large agricultural landowners were shifting their capital out of agriculture to industry, construction, and commerce. By the 1970s rates of return in industry were ten to fifteen percent higher than those in agriculture. Commercial farmers who remained in agriculture would have benefited from loans at favorable interest rates. The observation has been made that, overall, government policy seems to have discouraged "innovative peasant farmers" from increasing their investments.[9] In making loans, priority was given to well-capitalized enterprises over small farms.

AGRICULTURAL RECONSTRUCTION

Changes in the government's policies regarding landholding and management had an impact on agriculture probably equal to that of development financing. It has been suggested that it was characteristic of the

TABLE 8.2

Development Plans: Allocations to Agriculture
(billions of rials)

Category	Third Plan (1962-1967)	Fourth Plan (1968-1972)	Fifth Plan (1973-1978)
Total development expenditures	200	480	1,560
Agricultural development	45	65	208
Percentage for agriculture of total	22.5	13.5	18.3

Sources: Third Plan, p. 42; Fourth Plan, p. 23; Fifth Plan, p. 23.

Shah's approach to policymaking that technology and social engineering were preferred as instruments of change over political process. Agricultural policy in the 1960s and 1970s conforms to this impression. Land redistribution, for example, was approved during a period when the Shah had refused to convene parliament and was amended twice within six years.

Redistribution—the first reform. The Shah's close relationship with the United States directly and indirectly encouraged this outlook. The first national land redistribution program was initiated in 1962, with strong encouragement from President Kennedy. The Shah was interested in U.S. military assistance and the United States was pressing him to introduce economic reforms. An earlier and much weaker version of the bill had been passed by the previous parliament. Instead of working with parliament, the amended program went through by cabinet decree. The Shah's later criticisms of President Kennedy suggest that he would have preferred not to have pushed the issue through in that manner, although soon after he made land redistribution and the "White Revolution" the centerpiece of his regime.

The origins of the program resulted in a combination of provisions, somewhat hastily devised, that were not closely attuned to the needs of Iranian agriculture and the political realities of agricultural interests. Historically, farmlands were owned privately and by religious

TABLE 8.3

Development Expenditures:
Distribution Within Agricultural Sector
(millions of rials)

Type of program	Amount	Percentage of total
Irrigation	16.5	36.7
Land reform and cadastral survey	5.7	12.7
Agricultural credit	8.8	19.5
Training and research	1.0	2.2
Plant improvement programs	3.9	8.7
Conservation	1.6	3.6
Animal production	1.4	3.2
Commercial crops	1.1	2.4
Rural development	<u>5.0</u>	<u>11.4</u>
Total	45.0	100.0
Agricultural credits	14,000	21.5
Establishment of large agricultural units	11,000	16.9
Improvement of production and cultivation	7,000	10.8
Animal husbandry	7,000	10.8
Conservation	7,000	10.8
Agricultural services	6,500	10.0
Marketing	6,000	9.2
Research and studies	4,000	6.2
Land reform	<u>4,000</u>	<u>6.2</u>
Total	65,000	100.1
Preservation and exploitation of natural resources	12,650	13.6
Agro-industry	22,000	23.7
Raising agricultural output	9,200	10.0
Raising output of livestock produce	10,620	11.4
Agricultural services	7,210	7.8
Cooperatives and farm corporations	13,050	14.0
Regulation of the market of agricultural produce	12,500	13.4
Research and surveys	<u>5,700</u>	<u>6.2</u>
Total	93,000	100.1

Sources: *Third Plan*, p. 77, *Fourth Plan*, p. 115, *Fifth Plan*, p. 38.

foundations (the *oqaf*), the state, and the crown, or royal family. The re-distribution of crown and state lands had begun a decade before. In the first phase of the national redistribution, private landholdings and relig-ious endowments in excess of one village were to be transferred to the sharecroppers who had been working them. This was applied to all types of landholdings, including the religious lands. The former owners were to be reimbursed for their land at values determined by the taxes that they had previously paid.

In the second "phase" of land redistribution, landowners were given the option of leasing their land to sharecroppers under long-term (thirty-year) contracts. The third and final phase, announced in 1968, once again called on landowners with excess holding to sell their land or to distribute an amount of land to sharecroppers in proportion to the share of the produce that they had been receiving. Estimates of how many families received land during the three phases vary from 1.5 to 2.2 million.

An exception in the program was made for mechanized farms, orchards, and gardens. This decision was in keeping with the early pol-icy of mechanizing farming on state and crown lands.[10] Workers hired as seasonal labor were not eligible to receive land, a provision that was also compatible with the general direction of government policy toward large-scale, well-capitalized farming. In some respects it was the distribution of small parcels of land, symbolically the core of the program, that was not compatible. The small parcels were impossible to farm profitably and the former landowners' functions of providing seeds and fertilizer were not replaced by government programs in most cases. After land redistribu-tion, more than two million farmers in Iran were working an average of 1.7 hectares; they supplied forty percent of total agricultural production.

A system of producer cooperatives was set up soon after land re-distribution in order to make seeds, fertilizer, and machinery more avail-able. They also ran general stores in some places. By 1975 two-thirds of Iran's farm villages had formal cooperative structures, although they were not well financed. They also had management difficulties, which could be attributed, in part, to the government's ambivalence about peas-ant farming. One problem was that the farmers were often suspicious of management because it was responsible to local governors, who were themselves appointed by the Ministry of Interior. As a result, farmers regularly evaded the "two percent" tax which was levied to finance local development projects and collected by the cooperatives' local officers.[11] Finally, the Ministry of Cooperatives and Rural Development lost its independent status and was absorbed into the Ministry of Agriculture.

Farm corporations—the second reform. In 1968, just two years after the third phase of land redistribution was announced, a second, major initiative was undertaken—the creation of parastatal farms. The initiative was intended to respond to the problems of small plots that resulted from land redistribution. Farmers in that situation were encouraged to exchange their land for shares in a farm corporation in areas where they had been established.

Close to one hundred corporations were eventually set up. In order to attain this number, the government had to revise the original legislation to make it mandatory for all eligible farmers to join; the sanction against refusal was the expropriation of their land. Economically the program was a success, if the statistics on the corporations' performance are correct. After several years, farmers who joined corporations were earning higher incomes than they had when they were self-employed. The productivity of the farm corporations also was above average for the agricultural sector as a whole. Some opposition to the corporations persisted, however, on political grounds as they were seen as one more instance of state intervention in the private sector.

The "poles" policy—the third reform. In the wake of land redistribution and fragmentation, another, more radical, step was taken to reduce the number of marginal farms. The "Policy of Agricultural Development at the Poles of Soil and Water" was formulated by the then-minister of agriculture, Mansur Rouhani.[12] Its social and political implications were profound, although none of these were taken up in public debate. The policy called for moving entire village populations to the most fertile areas by attracting them with new government facilities. For that purpose the Fifth Plan funded 1,200 rural service centers, which would bring technical assistance and social and medical services to the selected areas. These would be areas that, according to government research, were found to have optimum water and soil conditions for farming.

The "target group" included most of the 4.5 million Iranians living in villages with populations of less than 250 persons.[13] Rural sociologists were critical of the poles policy on the ground that it disrupted traditional modes of production, particularly the *boneh*, a cooperative work group formed among individual peasants. Critics of the policy maintained that agricultural production, as well as community life, would be seriously affected by the breakdown of the *bonehs*. Yet despite the radical nature of the policy, those who were affected did not directly protest it. Rouhani, however, was executed by the Islamic government after the revolution.

Agribusiness—the fourth reform. The Shah was determined to modernize agriculture and did not believe that it could take place through small-scale peasant farming. From this perspective, the disruption caused by the poles policy was not a problem. The Ministry of Agriculture was instructed to promote agribusiness through preferential financing and by using eminent domain to allow them to take over the most well-irrigated land.

Many of the agribusinesses, defined as farms of over five thousand hectares, operated under thirty-year leases from the government. They were provided with land and water at subsidized prices. By the early 1970s agribusinesses were farming approximately 110,000 hectares, or 1.5 percent of Iran's total land area. They employed less than one percent of the agricultural work force and produced just two percent of the total agricultural output.[14]

The same "peasant lobby" that opposed the poles policy also opposed the policy of giving priority to agribusiness. In between were the medium-sized commercial farms that produced more than one third of agriculture's marketable surplus. These were also the farms that achieved the highest yields per acre.[15]

The most ambitious project and the beginning of agribusiness was the transformation of the Khuzistan region in the southwest of Iran, at the head of the Gulf. It was modeled after the Tennessee Valley Authority and promoted by David Lilienthal, the founder of the TVA. As a result of Lilienthal's recommendations to the Shah, a large hydroelectric dam was built on the Dez River and, below that, irrigation systems were installed. In 1968 the "Law for the Establishment of Companies for the Utilization of Lands Downstream From Dams" was enacted, which authorized the Ministry of Water and Power to take over all farmlands below major dams and to lease them to corporations that would engage in large-scale agricultural and/or animal husbandry operations.

Below the Khuzistan dam, about 100,000 hectares were to be put under mechanized production. Among the investors were Bank of America, John Deere, Shell International, Cotts, Chase Manhattan Bank, and Exxon. The largest enterprise, Iran-America, held 20,262 hectares; the smallest, 4,010 hectares. These holdings had previously been owned by individual farmers. Approximately seventeen thousand persons were displaced from the lands when the agribusinesses took over.[16]

The regime adopted agribusiness as a tool for improving animal husbandry as well. Part of the attraction of agribusiness was that it used modern animal husbandry techniques and part that it replaced tribal control of the industry. As a first step toward introducing animal husbandry enterprises, grazing land was nationalized and the numbers of grazing locations that nomadic herders could use were limited.

The state was directly involved in animal husbandry. The largest of the animal husbandry enterprises was the state-owned Moghan Agro-Industry, controlling thirteen thousand hectares in northwestern Iran with a feedlot capacity of 600,000 sheep.[17] Another state enterprise, the Industrial Meat Complex, was set up in 1976 at Marv Dasht in southwestern Fars province. Eventually, this complex was to include meat packing, canning, and carpet making.

Several projects were initiated in the private sector under franchises from U.S. corporations. Franchise agreements typically stipulated that growers would use imported stock, feed, and animal husbandry techniques. The government subsidized the purchase of imported feed and kept poultry prices at sufficiently high levels for producers to earn after-tax returns of as much as thirty percent.[18] In at least one case, the prerequisite set by the franchising company for concluding an agreement was that it would retain a share of the Iranian market for itself. Another cost imposed by this system was the breeders' dependence on imported feed. With the revolution, feed supplies were cut off and many breeders were forced to destroy their stock.

The government's investments in animal husbandry were very controversial. Some experts looked at Iran's scarcity of land and concluded that grazing was not an appropriate use. Bookers (U.K.) was commissioned to undertake a national cropping plan in 1975. The study stated that seventy percent of Iran's *irrigated* farmland would have to be used for fodder crops if Iran were to become self-sufficient in animal protein. This would mean that the main staples of the Iranian diet—wheat, oil, sugar, and rice—would have to be imported.

Despite Bookers's discouraging findings, the Ministry of Agriculture encouraged prospective investors, describing the twenty percent returns that they could realize in beef production. Much less optimistically, the U.S. Department of Commerce estimated returns of five percent and cautioned that a scarcity of water and of skilled management would hold down productivity.[19]

By 1976 eight hundred agribusiness corporations had been approved by the Ministry of Agriculture. Observing the government's commitment to large-scale farming, the U.S. Department of Commerce noted that manufacturers of agricultural machinery could look forward to a "nearly unlimited" market for their products. The value of agricultural machinery imported by Iran doubled from 1973 to 1975. The state-run Agricultural Development Machinery Organization also granted licenses to machinery producers to operate in Iran, and for a number of years, Deere (U.S.) held an exclusive license to make tractors there.

AGRICULTURAL GROWTH PROJECTIONS

According to agricultural economists, agricultural production would have been higher if the government had provided better financing. The government's own studies of Sixth Plan objectives indicated that agricultural growth was critical to the continued growth of the economy as a whole. Therefore, in the course of drafting the Fifth Plan, the Plan and Budget Organization tried to estimate the level of funding that would be required to substantially improve agricultural production. One estimate was based on the objective of achieving a seven percent growth rate in 1980.[20] To accomplish this, the government would have had to invest a minimum of $1.1 billion in agriculture every year. In contrast, the actual investment projected for the Fifth Plan was $.5 billion annually, or a total of $2.5 billion over the whole five-year period.

The difference between actual allotments during the Fifth Plan and the $1.1 billion estimate necessary for seven percent growth represented less than ten percent of the annual military budget. If the PBO estimates were accurate, a five percent annual reduction in military spending would have doubled the rate of growth in agricultural production and would have reduced the food import bill at the same time.

Other projections were made of the level of financing that would be necessary to alleviate rural poverty. Significantly narrowing the income gap between rural and urban workers was estimated to be far more costly than was the task of increasing agricultural production. One projection called for the expenditure of $23 billion by 1992, with another $155 billion required to create alternative jobs for unemployed and underemployed farm laborers. These sums were larger than the total military expenditures during the 1970s.

A shift in expenditures of such magnitude would not have occurred without a significant change in the political regime, and would have been unlikely even then. The Islamic regime attempted to reorient expenditures toward rural Iran, but it could not do so on such a massive scale. Still, the projections were useful because they made it clear that lack of financing was a real impediment to growth in agriculture and to progress in rural development. Investments were badly needed for projects like tertiary irrigation, feeder roads, improved crop varieties, extension services, and storage facilities.

SUMMARY

Agriculture was the slowest-growing sector in the economy. It could not successfully compete with industry, construction, and the military for government financing. One of the reasons was that the Shah was disaffected with Iran's traditional, rural society. His desire to build a modern Iran was encouraged by the views of Americans with whom he came into contact, both views that were solicited and those that were not. Through the U.S. relationship, the process of military modernization led to a policy that downgraded agriculture in substance as well as in financial terms.

When President Kennedy made military assistance contingent on socioeconomic reforms, a chain of events was set in motion that was characterized by a continuous, radical restructuring of farming from above, coupled with the steady upgrading of Iran's military establishment. This continued through three phases of land redistribution, new forms of farm organization, and a quasi-voluntary resettlement policy.

However, the money went elsewhere, with the exception of some sizable agribusiness development schemes, despite the evident need for basic services of all kinds. With more than a third of the population earning its livelihood from agriculture, the lack of productive employment was a serious problem. Urban migration resulted in a variety of social stresses; for many of those who remained, illiteracy, malnutrition, and disease were common.

Iran's land cannot be readily farmed. And, the population growth rate is at the heart of much rural poverty. These factors have little to do with the issue of military modernization. However, it is probable that agricultural production could have been increased if the regime had not invested so heavily in large-scale, mechanized farming. The alternative was to give more attention and funds to the medium-sized commercial farms that were producing for the market and the smaller subsistence farms that were supporting large numbers of people. Instead, imported technologies, organizational methods, and reconstruction strategies were preferred in agriculture as they were in the military and in industry.

NOTES

1. World Bank, *Study of Iran's Agricultural Economy* (1974), quoted in Theiry Brun and Rene Dumont, "Iran: Imperial Pretensions and Agricultural Dependence," *Merip Reports* 8, 8 (1978).

2. Ibid., p. 16.

3. World Bank, *World Development Report, 1979* (New York: Oxford University Press, 1979), p. 131.

4. Marvin G. Weinbaum, *Food, Development, and Politics in the Middle East* (Boulder, Col.: Westview Press, 1982), p. 31.

5. Oddvar Aresvik, *The Agricultural Development of Iran* (New York: Praeger, 1976), p. 261.

6. Iran, Ministry of Labor, General Department of Statistics, *Household Sample Survey 1970* (Teheran, 1971).

7. Weinbaum, *Food, Development, and Politics*, p. 31.

8. Personal interview.

9. Weinbaum, *Food, Development, and Politics*, p. 44.

10. Ibid., p. 81.

11. Shoko Okazaki, *The Development of Large-Scale Farming in Iran: The Case of the Province of Gorgan*, Occasional Papers 3 (Tokyo: Institute of Asian Economic Affairs, 1968).

12. These observations are based on field research on local politics undertaken in 1972 and 1973 in the Esfahan region. See Ann Schulz, *Local Politics and Nation-States: Case Studies in Politics and Policy* (Santa Barbara, Calif.: Clio Press, 1979).

13. Mansur Rouhani, *Towse'e eqtesadi dar qotbharje manabe'-ye ab va khak (Economic Development at the Poles of Soil and Water)* (Teheran: Ministry of Agriculture, 1967). The "poles policy" was similar to the "Ujaama" village program that was initiated by President

Nyerere's government in Tanzania in the 1960s, with the significant exception that force was not to be used to move people.

14. The 1966 national census, which was the last one to be published before the revolution, put the number of villages in Iran at 48,000.

15. Etienne Hirsch, *Employment and Income Policies for Iran* (Geneva: International Labour Office, 1973), p. 40.

16. Arsevik, *Agricultural Development*, p. 101.

17. Robert Graham, *The Illusion of Power* (New York: St. Martin's Press, 1978), p. 115.

18. The largest number of animals that were actually fed at Moghan was thirty thousand. The gap between expectation and performance in agribusiness is further discussed in Ann Schulz, "Food in Iran: The Politics of Insufficiency," in Raymond F. Hopkins et al., eds., *Food, Politics, and Agricultural Development* (Boulder, Col.: Westview Press, 1979): 171-192.

19. U.S. Department of Commerce, Domestic and International Business Administration, *Iran: A Survey of U.S. Business Opportunities* (Washington, D.C.: U.S. Government Printing Office, 1977), p. 26.

20. Iran, Plan and Budget Organization, *Sixth Plan Policy Questions* (Teheran: Planometrics and General Economy Bureau, Planning Division, June 1976).

NINE

Employment and Training

Employment and labor productivity were, and continue to be, critical issues in Iran, with a population that increases at an annual rate of about three percent. From 1956 to 1972 the population nearly doubled, rising from 19 million to 31 million. Whether a sufficient number of jobs are available is closely related to balanced economic growth and to problems of income distribution.[1] As we have seen, the low rate of growth in agriculture has led to rural poverty and high rates of urban migration.

The economic expansion that occurred after the mid-1960s included growth in capital-intensive industries which required skills that were scarce.[2] It has been suggested that military personnel programs can be beneficial to the economy as a whole by providing opportunities to learn new skills, as well as to improve worker productivity through general education and health care. As rapid changes in military technology occur, the military sector requires similar kinds of skills, which are expensive to provide. Is this training transferable to civilian jobs? Is it more efficient to provide the training indirectly in the military or directly in the civilian sector?

Few studies have been done of how military manpower policy actually affects employment in less industrial countries. Another possible benefit to the civilian economy from military expenditures on personnel is through the demand for consumer goods created by wage earners in the military. In countries which have chronic unemployment or underemployment, overall demand would be increased if the military draws from these groups or leaves civilian jobs open that they can enter. This chapter discusses these and other aspects of military employment in Iran.

131

THE STRUCTURE OF EMPLOYMENT IN IRAN

In the 1970s, agriculture still employed the largest number of Iranians. In 1966 forty-seven percent of the employed population reported that they worked in agriculture; by 1972 the percentage had risen to forty-nine.[3] Because agricultural work is more likely to be part-time and/or seasonal than other kinds of work, employment statistics for a work force that is predominantly agricultural can underestimate the numbers of people who are without work for substantial periods of time. The distinctions were apparent in Iran. In 1966, for example, the official unemployment figure was 3.7 percent.[4] The number rose to 9.6 percent when seasonal unemployment was included.[5] For 1971, the comparable figures were 2.4 and 11.1 percent.[6]

The labor force was growing at about 3.3 percent annually in the early 1970s, slightly faster than the population. According to official statistics, the growth in full-time employment exceeded that by about .4 percent.[7] This growth was taking place in the industrial and service sectors (which included government employment). The 1975 revised Fifth Plan anticipated that an estimated 40 percent of the two million new jobs created during the plan would be industrial, with 25 percent in construction and services. Within the industrial sector, most workers were employed in small shops with less than ten workers. In 1966, 85 percent of all industrial workers were so employed, despite the fact that the rate of growth in employment in larger establishments was three times that of employment in the small-scale enterprises over the previous decade.[8] In 1972 the percentage of industrial workers in small establishments had declined only 4 points, to 81.[9]

Along with the slow shift in employment from small to large-scale industries, the types of jobs being created in industry were undergoing a marked transformation. From 1956 to 1966, the number of persons employed in professional and technical occupations more than doubled.[10] By the time the Fifth Plan was revised, manpower projections projected the shortage of engineers at 44 percent of demand; that of technicians, 35.7 percent; and of skilled and semiskilled workers, 69 percent.[11] The cost of providing those jobs, including the cost of capital investment and training, was increasing as well.[12]

THE MILITARY AS EMPLOYER

This was the overall context within which military employment is to be seen. The military's ability to offer large numbers of jobs and to train people for work requiring technical skills was important if it was to supplement the needs of the civilian economy. Both of these requirements were met, although not necessarily as efficiently as they might have been using other approaches.

Military jobs were filled by the draft and by voluntary service. Compulsory military service for males was initiated in Iran in 1925; the number of persons employed by the military increased steadily thereafter. Despite American pressure to limit the number of troops, in the eight years from 1955 to 1963 the increase in personnel was over forty-seven percent (Table 9.1). The growth in military employment surpassed the rate of growth in employment in all other sectors. From the perspective of the total number of jobs needed, however, military employment looked less significant; it accounted for about two percent of the employed population.

One cross-national study found that there was greater income equality in countries that have high military participation rates.[13] From Iran's experience, it appears that the military did reach people who were likely to need full-time jobs. This can be inferred, for example, from the fact that the illiteracy rate in the armed forces was about fifty percent. This was a lower rate than that for the population as a whole, but higher than that of the male population. Information on the salaries enlisted men received was not published, but estimates placed them from $114 to $588 per month in the mid-1970s. Anywhere in that range, military salaries would have been higher than those received by rural workers, although lower than those received for skilled urban jobs.

Over the years from 1950 to 1977, the amount of money spent on salaries increased. From the mid-1960s on, personnel expenditures grew by nearly 70 percent every year, although they dropped from 69.5 to 12.8 percent of the total budget. The cost of each military job rose, however. In 1964 each military job represented $1,157 in personnel expenditures; in 1975, $21,653 in personnel expenditures purchased one job, which does not count capital expenditures. Civilian investments could create more jobs than could comparable investments in the military, although the same phenomenon of escalating capital costs was occurring in the civilian

TABLE 9.1

Size of Iran's Armed Forces, 1951-1980

Year	Total manpower	Percentage of increase
1951	151,000	
1955	136,000	-9.9
1959	177,000	30.1
1963	200,000	13.0
1967	210,000	4.8
1971	255,000	21.4
1975	385,000	51.0
1978	350,000	-9.1
1980	240,000	-3.1

Sources: Statesman's Yearbook (-1963); U.S. Arms Control and Disarmament Agency, *World Military Expenditures and Arms Transfers* (1963-); International Institute for Strategic Studies (London), *The Military Balance* (1980).

economy. Each job created under the Fifth Plan, for example, was estimated to cost $16,901, or twenty-two percent less than the military.[14]

The most striking distinction was not between the costs of military and civilian jobs but between public and private sector costs. New employment in the public sector involved far higher outlays per worker than did jobs in the private sector. Estimates for the period 1972 to 1977 showed investment levels of $4 million and $2.7 million, respectively. From these statistics, it appears that growth in private sector investment would have been the most effective way to meet Iran's employment needs in the short term.

From the mid-1960s on, the manpower requirements of the military became more diversified as the evolution of the separate services brought more specialization. By 1962 the air force and the navy had been established as independent entities, and they grew quickly over the next two decades (Table 9.2). The rapid acquisition of more complex weapons made it impossible to find Iranians to fill the jobs associated with the weapons. In 1977 a U.S. congressional study found sizable gaps in the ranks of the volunteer forces. Sixteen percent of the officers' positions in the army were vacant, thirty-one percent of the noncommissioned officers' positions, and forty-nine percent of the *homafars*, the technical specialists.[15]

TABLE 9.2

Distribution of Manpower Among Services

Year	Army	Air force	Navy	Gendarmerie
1951	130,000			21,000
1955	130,000			6,000
1959	150,000	5,000		22,000
1962	208,000	7,500	1,000	
1964	170,000	5,000		28,000
1967	164,000	10,000	6,000	25,000
1969	200,000	15,000	6,000	25,000
1974	175,000	50,000	13,000	70,000
1980	150,000	70,000	20,000	75,000

Sources: Statesman's Yearbook and *The Military Balance.*

As a result, although the number of jobs available in the military sector grew more rapidly than the population, many of the specialized jobs were filled with foreign nationals. Foreigners helped to train Iranian troops, to maintain and repair weapons, and to introduce new logistics and command systems. Before World War II, most foreign military advisers were working at the ministerial level. As the postwar military buildup proceeded, foreign participation became more specialized and extended deeper into the military establishment.[16] In 1978 approximately nine thousand U.S. nationals were working on military projects in Iran; of these, approximately seven thousand were employed by private weapons manufacturers. Two thousand technicians were working in Grumman-Iran's F-14 support program and in selling and servicing other Grumman weapons.[17] In that year, Bell Helicopter International hired 1,300 ex-servicemen to work on Bell projects in Iran.

This was a costly process. American military technicians earned from $2,500 to $3,500 per month, with supplementary compensation for "hardship duty." Often the fees received by the corporations that arranged the support services were three times the amount of the technicians' salaries. The salaries of U.S. technical support workers were higher than those of most Iranian military officers and also were higher than Iranian engineers' salaries at $1,700 to $2,000 per month.[18]

The economic effect of hiring foreign personnel was different from expenditures on salaries for Iranian personnel, particularly conscripts. One was that it reduced the multiplier effect on the domestic economy. Many foreign workers sent a portion of their earnings home. Some had commissary privileges of one kind or another and all had access to foreign goods. Those responsible for bringing in American workers described their job as trying to reproduce a life-style for those workers that would be as close as possible to that which they experienced in the United States. Another cost was additional inflationary pressure. The employment of foreign technicians contributed to the rising cost of housing in Teheran and Iranian officers could not find housing comparable to theirs.[19]

CIVILIAN TRAINING PROGRAMS

The civilian sector of Iran's economy was experiencing a similar labor shortage, particularly engineers and skilled technicians. In the mid-1970s, a shortage of unskilled laborers also developed. Here, too, foreign workers were brought in to fill the jobs. Altogether an estimated sixty thousand work permits were issued to foreign nationals in 1977, a three-fold increase over the two previous years;[20] over half of these were issued to Americans or Europeans. Engineers and technicians also were brought in from several Asian countries including Pakistan, India, South Korea, and the Philippines. In the mid-1970s, unskilled laborers from Afghanistan, Pakistan, Iraq, and Bahrain came to Iran and worked there without permits. By the time of the revolution, as many as one million foreign workers were employed in Iran.[21]

Shortages of skilled workers were a function of the pace at which new technology was being introduced. The financial incentives to develop technical skills were there: according to a survey conducted by the Ministry of Labor, the wages of skilled workers were ten times higher than those of unskilled workers.[22] However, historically, technical and mechanical skills were not highly valued and therefore training facilities had not been made available.

To respond to the shortages, the national development plans spelled out goals for increasing state-funded scientific and technical education programs. The largest growth in vocational training capacity occurred at the secondary school level. Between the beginning of the Second and Third plans, the number of secondary students increased by 95.9

percent and that of vocational students by 88.9 percent.[23] Then, under the Third Plan, adult technical training was introduced by the Ministry of Labor. Over the next five years (1962-1967), 3,900 workers were trained.

It was decided that the Fourth Plan would bring together vocational and academic programs in the secondary schools, whose curricula were criticized as "too theoretical."[24] The goal was to graduate 46,000 persons from the new combined program by 1972, when the plan ended. According to figures published in the Fifth Plan, that objective was met and surpassed. The summary of accomplishments shown in the plan document is as follows: post-high school vocational students rose from 17,000 (1968) to 24,700 (1972); 64,550 high school vocational students were graduated; and, 31,050 students attended adult vocational programs (see Table 9.3).[25] In total, 2.2 billion rials ($33,000) was allocated to vocational and technical training under the plan.[26]

The Fifth Plan itself called for continuing growth in vocational enrollments, with the objective of meeting half of the demand for technical graduates at the secondary level. Funding for all levels of technical/vocational training was set at 44 billion rials, or about $620,000.[27] This was an enormous increase over the Fourth Plan, although in interviews, officials who were responsible for training institutes voiced the opinion that the level of funding was unsatisfactory if they were to make a serious effort to meet the shortages of technical skills. Per graduate, the costs of vocational training were very low. If the plan objective of training 804,000 persons were met, the expenditure per person would be less than $1,000.

The courses were not to be limited to industrial skills; fields of study were also to include health and social services, handicrafts, commercial subjects, and administrative training. Almost one-third of the students in the secondary school vocational training programs were women; by that time it was not unusual to find women working in textile, handicraft, and electronics workshops.

Higher education in science and engineering presented a different situation. Many Iranians went abroad for education at this level; in the mid-1970s from 40,000 to 53,000 Iranians were studying abroad annually.[28] Of those Iranians studying abroad, eighty-one percent were taking scientific courses, as compared with forty-nine percent of those studying in Iran.[29] Many of these students were receiving state financing, a policy that the Islamic regime has continued although to a lesser extent.

TABLE 9.3

Vocational Training Enrollments

	Secondary voc.-tech. 1968-1973		Voc. adult and post-sec. 1968-1973	Military–U.S. assisted 1964-1977
Civilian	17,000	64,550	55,750	
Military			6,960[a]	139[b]

Sources: Fourth Plan, p. 268; *Fifth Plan,* p. 125; U.S. House of Representatives, Committee on International Relations, *The Persian Gulf, 1975: The Continuing Debate on Arms Sales,* Hearings before a Special Subcommittee on Investigations (Washington, D.C.: U.S. Government Printing Office, 1977), p. 252.
[a]This figure is an annual average. The total for the Fifth Plan was 34,800.
[b]Total military training under MAP, IMETP, and MFS over thirteen years was 22,000.

One of the problems of sending students abroad was that a significant proportion did not return to Iran. Available statistics show that thirty percent of those who went abroad for scientific and medical training did not return.[30] To respond to this problem, the Shah encouraged the establishment of research facilities in Iran and higher salaries for returning professionals.

MILITARY TRAINING

There were four types of military training program in Iran, one of which was directly applicable to the civilian sector. The four types were: induction and literacy classes; training for general officers at four military colleges in Iran and through foreign programs; technical training programs that instructed personnel with the special rank of *homafar* in the maintenance, repair, and use of specific weapons and weapons systems; and vocational training, offered to a limited number of conscripts during their last three months of military duty.

In 1975 the military provided training for about 9,500 persons, including the vocational courses which were offered to an estimated 7,000 recruits. Overall, this number amounted to about ten percent of the numbers enrolled in civilian technical schools and in-service training programs.[31] Vocational training included courses in farming, welding, carpentry, and plumbing.[32] According to official figures, from 1962 to 1967 some 34,800 servicemen took one of these courses. In that period the size of the army grew from 160,000 to 200,000 persons, of whom two-thirds were conscripts. Assuming a biannual turnover of thirty percent among the conscripts, the vocational courses probably could have reached a maximum of twenty percent of the total number of service leavers.

Apparently, no surveys were undertaken of the postmilitary employment experiences of veterans. An example from Korea illustrates the possibility that people may not use their training when they return to civilian life: two-thirds of those who had received technical training in the military eventually returned to farming rather than to industrial jobs.[33] Iran's situation, however, was very different because there were few agricultural jobs. A combination of anecdotal evidence and migration data suggests that military service was one avenue through which urban migration took place and that there was a potential for using the vocational courses that prepared veterans for technical jobs.

Military-specific technical training was different. It was carried out primarily by foreigners, and most often by Americans. About half of this training was in the handling, maintenance, and repair of specific weapons. For many years, the U.S. government trained Iranian military personnel under the Military Assistance Program. When military assistance was phased out in the late 1960s, the Iranian government contracted for training under the International Military Education and Training Program. Altogether, an estimated 22,000 Iranians received training under these two programs from 1964 to 1977.[34]

A congressional review of U.S. military training programs was undertaken in 1976. Its report put 61 percent of trainees in the category of maintenance and communications/electronics.[35] An Iranian air force study estimated that by 1977, 1,500 maintenance personnel had been trained for the F-5E/F program and 5,300 for the F-4.[36] Of these, about twenty-five percent were skilled specialists and another fifty percent were technicians. This represented about half the total number of technicians that were needed to maintain the aircraft that Iran had acquired at that time.[37]

With each new acquisition came the need for additional training. What makes this noteworthy is that each training contract involved a large outlay of funds in proportion to Iran's total military budget. According to U.S. figures, military training carried out in just one year

(1975) under contract with American providers cost $298,652,000.[38] With 2,674 Iranians in training, the cost per person works out to approximately $100,000.

The cost of specialized military training was very high compared to civilian courses. According to the 1975 figures, military training cost one hundred times the amount required to bring someone through a civilian vocational/technical program (see figures above). We do not know how much of this kind of training was useful in nonmilitary jobs. According to interviews with Americans who participated in the training, most of the technical skills that were taught covered very rudimentary repair functions, such as interpreting malfunction indicators. At this level of specificity, the potential spillover of the training was probably not very great.[39] On the other hand, the fact that both military and civilian employers complained about the loss of trained technicians to the other sector indicates that some spillover was occurring.

MILITARY SERVICE AND LABOR ATTITUDES

Military service has been described as a process that contributes to nationalism and positive attitudes toward modernization, both of which could, in turn, foster increased labor productivity and economic growth.[40] An article written in the mid-1960s about the effects of military conscription in Iran argued that military service did break down ethnic barriers and produce a sense of shared nationality among soldiers who worked together.[41]

Ethnicity has been a frequent source of conflict in Iran and a salient factor in military policies.[42] Iran's armed forces were used more inside its borders than outside and almost always against ethnic minorities. Historically, the Iranian military was itself relatively homogeneous, made up almost entirely of ethnic Persians and Azeri Turks.[43] Conscription changed this somewhat, but the leadership ranks still overrepresented those two groups.

Against the record of the military as permeated by ethnic politics, there is only anecdotal evidence that it was a "melting pot" and strengthened nationalism in an economically productive way. In Iran, the fairly recent identification with the nation may have raised the intensity of conflict over economic and political issues as they became more relevant to all Iranians.

The relationship between military service and positive attitudes toward modernization also is ambiguous. Like the military "melting pot" process, modernization has a political dimension. In Iran, the military experience of many promoted hostility toward westernization, which was interpreted in such a way that military technology was the only aspect of modernization that was deemed acceptable. Military personnel were constantly aware of the U.S. presence, since it was presumably more visible to them than to any other group of Iranians, and since they were expected to conform their behavior to U.S. military customs. One outcome of this experience was that members of the armed forces who were exposed to modern training and ideas rejected the political context that provided them and became part of the opposition to the Shah's regime. Several former *homafars*, for example, became prominent leaders in the underground *mujaheddin* when they left the service. In another instance, one of the first military rebellions in the revolution was led by a group of air force *homafars*.

The earlier view that the military was a modernizing institution in the Third World has begun to give way to more empirically based observations that the military may be one of the most conservative, or reluctant to change.[44] Empirical studies of military organizations raise another question about the modernization hypothesis in its suggestion that a "work ethic" prevails in the military or that efficiency is distinctly valued. In one study of the Indian military, for example, the researcher found a list of attitudes that were the converse: "corruption, inefficiency, low morale, slothfulness," and others.[45]

SUMMARY

Iranian workers needed more jobs, more productive jobs, and training appropriate to existing and future work opportunities. Most Iranians during the period that we are focusing on were working in agriculture, small-scale industry, services, and construction. New employment opportunities were being created in industry that required technical skills at all levels. The questions that needed to be asked about manpower policies, then, were: were they providing jobs directly, were they contributing to raising the productivity of workers in their present jobs (i.e., farming and cottage industries), and were they providing training for new types of employment?

Military expenditures on personnel did provide jobs and training for thousands of Iranians. The military did not absorb all the unemployed workers, but the number that it did employ grew rapidly during the 1960s and 1970s. Given the changes in the types of jobs that were available in the military with the weapons buildup, many more Iranians could have found employment there had they received technical training earlier in the process. Instead, the arms buildup brought in foreigners with those skills from the West, and from Asia to fill the shortages that existed, so that in effect this portion of Iranian military expenditures were creating jobs that contributed to employment for nationals of other countries rather than increasing domestic employment.

The cost of importing technical skills was high both in terms of the salaries that had to be offered to Americans to get them to go to Iran and in terms of the inflationary effect that they had on the cost of living. To reduce future manpower shortages, technical training programs were offered to members of the Iranian military. Much of this training was contracted for as part of weapons acquisition packages and it, too, was expensive.

Similar shortages of technical skills existed in the civilian economy. The Shah's decision simultaneously to enlarge Iran's arsenal of advanced weapons and to industrialize created competition between the military and civilian sectors for technical skills. Many more people were being reached through civilian training programs, which also were less costly. Military technical training could be described as supplementing civilian programs, but not much more. Weapon-specific training probably had only limited applicability to other types of technical jobs.

The most innovative use of military funds for training was the vocational courses that were offered to conscripts before they left the service. These courses apparently did attempt to increase skills and, therefore, productivity in areas in which veterans were likely to find employment—farming, mechanics, small manufacturing.

Such different types of training activities that were undertaken by the military in Iran would undoubtedly be found in other countries. The usefulness of the conclusions that we draw about the benefits of military personnel expenditures for employment and productivity in the economy as a whole surely depends on learning more about the specific types of training that are offered and on looking at the issue of the employment of foreign nationals. Iran's experience in these two areas indicates that the manpower implications of rapid arms buildup warrant serious attention.

This conclusion is supported by the impact of military service on attitudes. Reactions within the military to the presence of foreign nationals and to their Western training showed how nationalism and modernization can interact to affect attitudes in ways that are quite contrary to social scientists' initial expectations about the military experience. Military service does not necessarily produce a "modernized and nationalistic" work force, one devoid of overriding political orientation. Both concepts include a range of attitudes that influence labor productivity, from xenophobic nationalism and political intolerance to the interest in using new technology. The personnel serving in Iran during the 1960s and 1970s may or may not have been more willing and capable workers; they do appear to have been more politicized and willing soldiers.

NOTES

1. Jiri Skolka and Michel Garzuel, *Changes in Income Distribution, Employment, and Structure of the Economy: A Case Study of Iran*, working paper for the Income Distribution and Employment Programme (Geneva: International Labour Office, 1976).

2. Inequality was an important issue in Iran during the 1970s. Expenditure data for the sample year 1971 showed that the top income deciles accounted for fifty-six percent of all consumer expenditures. Ibid., p. 85.

3. F. Aminzadeh, "Human Resources Development: Problems and Prospects," in Jane W. Jacqz, *Iran: Past, Present and Future* (New York: Aspen Institute for Humanistic Studies, 1976), p. 190.

4. Ibid., p. 181.

5. Etienne Hirsch, *Employment and Income Policies for Iran* (Geneva: International Labour Office, 1973), p. 27.

6. Iran, Plan and Budget Organization, Statistical Centre of Iran, *Statistical Yearbook of Iran, 1973-74* (Teheran, June 1976), p. 38.

7. Hirsch, *Employment and Income Policies*, p. 30.

8. William H. Bartsch, *Problems of Employment Creation in Iran*, Employment Research Papers (Geneva: International Labour Office, 1970).

9. Rostam Kavoosi, "Structural Change in the Iranian Manufacturing Industry, 1959-1972," unpublished doctoral dissertation, Harvard University, 1976, p. 89.

10. Bartsch, *Problems of Employment Creation*, p. 15.

11. Aminzadeh, "Human Resources," p. 192.

12. Hirsch, *Employment and Income Policies*, p. 54.

13. Erich Weede and Horst Tiefenbach, "Some Recent Explanations of Income

Inequality," *International Studies Quarterly* 25, 2 (June 1981): 255-282.

14. Hirsch, *Employment and Income Policies*, p. 54.

15. U.S. House of Representatives, Committee on International Relations, *United States Arms Policies in the Persian Gulf and Red Sea Areas: Past, Present, and Future*, Report of a Staff Survey Mission to Ethiopia, Iran, and the Arabian Peninsula, December 1977 (Washington, D.C.: U.S. Government Printing Office, 1977).

16. E.A. Bayne and R.O. Collin, "Arms and Advisors: Views From Saudi Arabia and Iran," *Southwest Asia Series 19*, American Universities Field Staff (1976).

17. *New York Times*, January 21, 1975.

18. Gail Cook Johnson, *High-Level Manpower in Iran* (New York: Praeger, 1980), p. 16.

19. *Forbes*, March 1, 1975; Hossein Razavi and Firouz Vakil, *The Political Environment of Economic Planning in Iran, 1971-1983* (Boulder, Col.: Westview Press, 1984), p. 87.

20. Johnson, *High-Level Manpower*, p. 16.

21. *Nouvel Observateur*, July 9, 1979.

22. Johnson, *High-Level Manpower*, p. 16.

23. Iran, Plan and Budget Organization, *Fourth National Development Plan* (Teheran: Organization, 1968), p. 268.

24. Ibid., p. 266.

25. Iran, Plan and Budget Organization, *Iran's Fifth Development Plan 1973-1978* (Teheran: Organization, 1973), p. 125.

26. *Fourth National Development Plan*, p. 281.

27. *Iran's Fifth Development Plan*, p. 127.

28. Nader Fatahi and Stig Ericsson, *Migrationes Iranicae* (Sweden, Institute of Sociologies, University of Lund, December 1976).

29. Johnson, *High-Level Manpower*, p. 42.

30. Fatahi, *Migrationes Iranicae*, p. 42.

31. *Iran's Fifth Development Plan*, p. 123.

32. Richard F. Nyrop, ed., *Iran: A Country Study* (Washington, D.C.: U.S. Government Printing Office, 1978), p. 411.

33. Korea University, Labor Education and Research Institute, *Economic Development and Military Technical Manpower of Korea: A Study of Manpower Development in the Military of Korea* (Seoul: Korea University Press, 1976).

34. Stephanie Neuman, "Security, Military Expenditures and Socioeconomic Development," *Orbis* 22, 3 (Fall, 1978); 589, quoting from U.S. Department of Defense, *Foreign Military Sales and Military Assistance Facts* (Washington, D.C.: U.S. Government Printing Office, 1977).

35. U.S. House of Representatives, Committee on International Relations, *The Persian Gulf, 1975: The Continuing Debate on Arms Sales*, Hearings before a Special Subcommittee on Investigations (Washington, D.C.: U.S. Government Printing Office, 1975), p. 252.

36. Stephanie Neuman, *Unravelling the Triad: Arms Transfers, Indigenous Defense Production, and Dependency—Iran as an Example* (Washington, D.C.: Department of State, Foreign Affairs Research Documentation Center, 1979), p. 19.

37. Ibid.

38. U.S. House of Representatives, Committee on International Relations, *The Persian Gulf, 1975*, p. 252.

39. Personal interviews, and Bayne and Collin, "Arms and Advisors."

40. Morris Janowitz, *Sociology and the Military Establishment*, 3rd ed. (Beverly Hills, Calif.: Sage Publications, 1974); Lucian W. Pye, "The Army in Burmese Politics," in John J. Johnson, ed., *The Role of the Military in Underdeveloped Countries* (Princeton: Princeton University Press, 1962).

41. Leo Hamon, ed., *Le Role Extra-Militaire de l'Armee Dans le Tiers Monde* (Paris: Centre d'Etudes des Relations Politiques, Université de Dijon, 1966).

42. Ann T. Schulz, "Iran: State-Building and the Defense Community," paper delivered to the Section on Military Studies, International Studies Association, November 1978.

43. Alvin J. Cottrell and Frank Bray, *Military Forces in the Persian Gulf*, Washington Papers 6 (Washington, D.C.: Center for Strategic and International Studies, Georgetown University, 1978).

44. Saadet Deger, "The Developmental Effect of Military Expenditure in LDCs," paper prepared for Colloque on Armement-Developpment-Droits de l'Homme-Desarmement, University of London, October 29, 1982.

45. R. Tapar, "State of the Military," *The Statesman Weekly*, September 19, 1981.

TEN

Conclusion

Today, millions of human beings live in poverty. And, today, governments spend billions of dollars on weapons and military personnel. These two facts come together to create one of the major policy issues of our time: how can we provide for the essentials of human dignity and security in a world of conflict? The basic premise of this study is that the optimum level of military spending is that which causes the least economic hardship while responding realistically to potential military threats. To state the premise in this way is to recognize that the most useful policy conclusions from a study of this topic are likely to be incremental ones and need to be based on a review of both military security and economic policies. Kodzic has described this approach as opportunity cost analysis.[1] Realistically, such analysis must be extended beyond the "standards of economic efficiency" that Kodzic recommends to include standards of political effectiveness, too. Politics helps both to explain the origins of security and economic decisions and to determine the outcomes of those decisions.

MILITARY EXPENDITURES AND ECONOMIC PERFORMANCE

In historical terms, Iran's military expenditures from the end of World War II to 1978 were not exceptionally high relative to total spending. The proportion of the state budget that was spent on the military was higher at the beginning of the century than it was in the 1970s, although the absolute amounts were greater. State revenues grew dramatically during the 1960s and 1970s, and military spending kept pace with overall government expenditures. Military spending over the century varied from about ten percent to fifty percent of the state budget. Periods of relatively low military spending were characterized by several factors: low security threat levels (the 1930s under Reza Shah); financial constraints (the war years and the early 1950s); and external pressures (the late 1950s).

At the most superficial level of analysis, apart from the question of optimizing security and growth, the economic record does not suggest a fundamental conflict between military spending and growth. Even during the 1970s, when military spending was very high, the annual growth rate was over five percent. However, when a time lapse was included to allow for a reaction period, a negative relationship between military spending and economic growth appeared.

Neither private capital formation nor industrial growth rates seemed to be adversely affected by military spending increases; both were positive throughout the periods of high military spending. In fact, capital formation increased even more rapidly *with* increased military spending when a time lapse was included in the analysis. Industrial growth, however, did not bring with it an increase in domestic value added for most industries. In fact, the mid-1970s were marked by a flight of capital from the country and by a slight downturn in industrial investment and production.

The economic gains that were achieved during the 1960s and 1970s were not evenly distributed throughout the economy. Agriculture exhibited the poorest growth rates of any sector. Rural incomes were much lower than in the urban sector, and the gap was widening. This was one area that clearly could have benefited from a reallocation of government spending. Funding was badly needed for small-scale infrastructure, such as tertiary irrigation and feeder roads. The military provided jobs and some training for many young people from rural areas, but not enough to avert massive urban migration or to alleviate the underlying structural problems that resulted in unemployment and underemployment.

The kind of political (and, therefore, financial) commitment to broad-based development that would have improved the status of the rural poor was not there. Public investments could have helped to counterbalance the effects of economic and technological dualism. However, development spending declined, not increased, as military expenditures rose—even though some military expenditures were included in the development budget.

THE NATURE OF MILITARY EXPENDITURES

Military spending is a composite; aggregate expenditures do not describe the actual purchases that are made nor how those change over time. However, the economic impact of military spending is determined by what is bought for the military and from whom, as well as by how much is spent on it. Seeing what is bought from whom also brings political issues into focus. Although the hypothetical economic benefits to be derived from military spending that some people talk about assume a politically neutral environment, their interaction in Iran was not determined by an "invisible hand" alone, but by deliberate decisions based on politics and ideology.

The lesson from Iran is that political factors can have a determining effect on the extent to which military spending, per se, contributes to or detracts from economic growth. The single most important characteristic of Iran's military expenditures in the late 1960s was that, in accordance with the Shah's military security policies, weapons procurement became the largest item in the budget, replacing personnel costs. Before that time, and ever since the first figures on military spending were published, salaries accounted for well over half of all military expenditures. The shift took place very rapidly. And, along with these weapons purchases came major expenditures for constructing facilities for their maintenance, repair, and eventual production. Most of these— weapons, technology, engineering skills, and the capital and intermediate goods they required—were imported.

This development carried with it several implications for the economy. First, others have suggested that military spending could potentially benefit the civilian economy by producing a demand for consumer goods from military employees and for intermediate and capital goods from military production. These effects were reduced, however, when the larger share of the military budget was going neither to salaries nor to purchase goods domestically. The shift from a *manpower* military to a *weapons-intensive* military also meant that income from personnel expenditures was transferred from foot soldiers to engineers and technicians, many of whom had to be brought from abroad.

Civilian industrialization was affected in other ways, too, by the change in military priorities. Military imports were increasing at the same time that industrial demand for imported intermediate and capital goods was increasing. The military and civilian industries also were competing for technically-skilled labor. Although many workers trained during their military service did go into civilian industries, their military training was vastly more expensive than that which could have been provided in civilian programs.

The problem of competition between the military and civilian industries was exacerbated by the fact that relatively few private sector firms were involved in military enterprises. One reason was the kind of technology that was being purchased and the absence of domestic capability to produce the military goods that the Shah wanted. Traditional industry received less and less support from development funds and virtually none from military spending, which only widened the rift between the Shah's regime and traditional groups in the population. Even when the expertise was there, however, the Shah was reluctant to ask private sector firms to participate in military projects. Instead, he placed the facilities under the direct control of the state and hand-picked trusted individuals as managers.

DEVELOPMENT AND SECURITY

Even though civilian industry was not invited to participate in producing all types of goods for the military, total industrial production still increased in Iran at the same time that military expenditures did. What the industrial production figures do not show, however, is how much of this production was state production of military goods. From the few available statistics that do differentiate between military and civilian projects in industrial investment (see Chapter 7), it can be concluded that the military accounted for a significant portion of industrial production (perhaps an increasing one).

When military production sets the parameters for the industrial sector as a whole, the product may be something more akin to "remotely-piloted butter" than to guns and butter. How the nature of modern military technology will influence the industrialization process in the less industrial countries is an open question. Given the costly and sophisticated technology that is now available, there is no reason to assume that military investments will help to bring about consumer-oriented industrialization as they did in the West much earlier.[2]

In Iran, the civilian markets for the goods produced in the interests of military modernization were not well developed. Such products as nuclear power, advanced telecommunications, electronic equipment, or aircraft design had few applications to civilian needs. Another way in which military expenditures affected industrial development during the 1970s was that the government adopted a policy of promoting export industries in response to the high import requirements of the military sector. Previously, industrial development had centered around import substitution and production for domestic markets.

Given the pervasiveness of poverty in Iran, the traditional structure of its industries, and the major role of agriculture as a provider of employment, long-term growth could probably have been higher if military spending had been reduced and *if* the resources saved had been invested in productive ways. The quality of life of Iranians living in poverty certainly could have been improved, and that would almost certainly have contributed to overall productivity.

A subtle political dimension of adopting a security policy that used oil revenues to buy imported weapons was that the Shah did not have to negotiate with the private sector or with taxpayers to get the weapons that he wanted. This situation was quite different from weapons procurement during the industrialization process in Europe and America, where governments had no alternative but to rely on domestic products.

Could military expenditures have been reduced marginally in order to support these goals without taking any major security risks? Were there specific types of expenditures which were of marginal importance to security? Were there alternative approaches to improving security which would have entailed different kinds of expenditures?

There is little question that Iran's security environment was a potentially hostile one. The country's strategic location and resources made it an arena for competition among the world's most powerful states. Political turmoil in the region became enmeshed in great-power politics and heightened the possibility of military conflict among local states. And, finally, the fragility of Iran's domestic political consensus meant that national security decisions were intertwined with the strategies to promote the security of the political regime—a key factor in Iran's security policy.

It is the conclusion of this study, however, that changes in military spending could have been made without taking major security risks.

The potential threat from Iraq, singularly and as a Soviet client, was a primary explanation offered for the armaments programs carried out under the Shah. Yet there is no evidence that additional weapons acquisitions during the period of the most rapid arms buildup actually increased the country's military capabilities proportionally; and several former government officials have expressed their doubts on this score.

The weapons acquisitions did not ensure Iran's security vis-à-vis Iraq. In the calculus of the Iraqi decision to invade Iran in 1980, perceived political instability in Iran outweighed the deterrent factor of Iran's weapons. It is true that American support had ended by then, but President Saddam Hussein apparently expected Iran's defense to collapse because of lack of support for the Islamic government. Partly from necessity and partly because it has a strong political foundation in the community, the Islamic regime has returned to a "labor-intensive" military policy, dependent on the *pasdaran* and the irregular *bassij*. This has been sufficient to defend Iranian territory, although it has not permitted Iran to achieve its offensive objectives.

Simply reducing military expenditures in the absence of other activities will not automatically bring about lower levels of security or higher rates of growth. Had the political components of security been weighed more heavily during the monarchy, and had they been backed up with more financial support for development programs, it is quite possible that Iran's national security would have been increased, rather than lessened, with less military spending.

THE EVOLUTION OF THE ARMS BUILDUP AND ECONOMIC REFORM

In the course of looking at the military budget and what was bought, by whom, and from whom, the most apparent links with security policy are the Shah's decisions to respond to the range of security threats that Iran faced through maintaining a close military relationship with the United States. This relationship began with internal politics and American assistance in consolidating the Shah's hold on the army. It eventually extended to regional politics and the Shah's assertion of an active military and diplomatic role for Iran.

The Shah's approach to economic modernization was not an alternative to the arms buildup; it was cut from the same cloth. Policies grow through accretion. The formation of Iran's military posture occurred through years of bargaining for U.S. military assistance. It was a reciprocal process of negotiations and decisions that encompassed economic policies as well as the nature of military development.

In the process of acquiring the military support that he wanted, the Shah was encouraged to take steps to reform the economy, for U.S. policy was that reform was the appropriate response to the challenge of communism. When the Shah first agreed to introduce the national land redistribution plan, the United States began to provide assistance for more elaborate military modernization programs. The two strategies converged ominously in June 1963, when anti-land reform demonstrations, in which Khomeini was instrumental, brought troops into the streets on the same day that an American adviser arrived to begin constructing a counterinsurgency force for the Shah.

Nevertheless, the Shah seized upon the idea of mandating economic change through state intervention as the raison d'etre of his regime and Iran's opportunity to catch up with the West. This attitude was nowhere more evident than in agricultural policy. Within a period of less than twelve years: grazing land was nationalized; three phases of land redistribution were carried out (not all of which were complementary); state farm corporations were first offered to and then imposed on small farmers in some regions; a village relocation ("poles policy") was initiated; and a policy of strong support for agribusiness was adopted and implemented.

While these experiments in economic and social engineering were being carried out, the military relationship between Iran and the United States became more weapons oriented. In explanation of the new reality, the concept of Iran as "second-order power" emerged. By the early 1970s, Iran came to be regarded as a modernizing nation with a rapidly developing military capability that was compatible with Western interests in most respects. From the standpoint of international politics, it was a period of relative stability and of positive diplomatic initiatives.

Within the country, however, these developments sowed political discord and economic uncertainty. State planning left little room for small-scale rural development programs, for traditional industries, for the bazaar economy (where the United States alliance also happened to be unpopular), or for putting the interests of the private sector ahead of government when the need for fiscal restraint arrived. The failure to achieve balanced economic growth in Iran under the monarchy cannot be attributed solely to military spending. Among the factors discussed in this study are the scarcity of productive land, the historically heavy hand of the state in economic activity, and timing (being a relative latecomer to industrialization). But the Shah's military policies, which determined the form that military spending would take, did little to overcome this legacy.

In fact, in Iran's experience, the concept of military-led economic growth was probably less relevant than that of economic-growth-led military development—i.e., that military capability ultimately depends on a solid economic and political foundation. This suggests that there is no simple remedy—such as weapons purchases—for insecurity, and that earlier, more comprehensive concepts of national power, including a sense of political community and economic resilience, were also more realistic.

POLICY ISSUES

Policy choices were available during the 1960s and 1970s had the politics of policymaking encouraged the Shah to reassess Iran's security needs and resources in a broader context. By taking advantage of the opportunity to look at Iran's experience retrospectively, future military assistance and sales policies could be improved. The most obvious issues in Iran's case involved (1) the content of military purchases; (2) the timing of military purchases; (3) who suppliers were to be; and (4) what role internal politics would have in supporting national security policy. One example of the content alternatives was whether to acquire the most sophisticated weapons for the military as rapidly as possible (the "matching Iraq" alternative, which was adopted) or to exercise selectivity (a "regional defensive" posture). In addition to reducing expenditures, the latter option would have had the advantage of limiting the United States' presence that was so visible and that fostered political conflict.

The timing of military purchases is also a potentially significant policy decision. Rapid changes in the amount or distribution of government spending can increase uncertainty among private sector investors in the form of access to state development funds, foreign exchange, and competition for capital goods. Staggered purchasing helps to alleviate these pressures, and allows more time for integrated military development.

Political process is a central issue in the economic effect of military spending. The Shah's failure to solidify the political foundation of his regime made it difficult for him to use military funds to benefit the civilian economy. This, too, was his choice—to engage in politics at home or instead to seek weapons and allies abroad. Many of the more harmful (or less beneficial) effects of military spending resulted from political decisions, not from an inevitable clash between military security and economic growth.

NOTES

1. Peter Kodzic, "Armaments and Development," in David Carlton and C. Shaeffers, eds., *The Dynamics of the Arms Race* (New York: Wiley, 1975), pp. 202-230.

2. Asbjorn Eide, "The Transfer of Arms to Third World Countries and Their Internal Uses," *International Social Science Journal* 28, 2 (1976): 308; Jagat S. Mehta, ed., *Third World Militarization* (Austin: University of Texas Press, 1984), p. 54.

Appendices

Official Budgets: State, Government, Military
(billions of current rials)

Year	State budget	Government budget	National defense	(current 1975)	National defense and internal security
1948	7.15		1.72		
1949	11.11		2.48	7.08	
1950	11.47		2.48	7.08	
1951	10.15		3.43	9.80	
1952	5.		1.58	4.51	
1953	12.27		2.55	7.29	
1954	13.05		5.24	1.83	
1955	13.59		4.91	17.19	
1956	18.35		5.87	20.55	6.92
1957	21.94	20.88	5.88	20.58	6.98
1958	29.22	29.	10.15	35.53	11.43
1959	65.26		8.22	28.77	
1960	83.18	78.89	9.65	27.72	11.26
1961	57.00		14.14	42.46	
1962	59.15		12.50	37.99	16.30
1963	55.15		12.64	38.89	14.86
1964	144.44	94.30	13.77	40.86	16.43
1965	176.66	113.30	18.10	54.35	21.19
1966	192.11	126.56	19.84	59.75	23.61
1967	217.23	141.98	28.20	85.71	32.45
1968	274.58	189.45	36.74	109.67	41.61
1969	330.30	221.77	44.49	132.41	49.75
1970	392.45	280.98	58.65	173.82	64.43
1971	454.30	315.80	78.60	218.94	
1972	548.50	386.90	100.90	263.45	
1973	824.30	598.80	142.20	253.03	151.90
1974		1603.40	372.80	418.88	389.70
1975	2470.00	1803.50	525.50	525.50	546.00
1976	3084.70	2063.80	561.10	509.25	591.90
1977	3530.00	2390.20	561.10	435.64	591.90

Sources: Most of the early figures are from *Statesman's Yearbook* and SIPRI; from 1955 on, the military data is from official budgets and from 1963 on, all data is official Iranian data.

Iran's Military Servicing and Production Contracts
(pre-1978)

	Activity	Location
Missile systems:		
1. Hughes Aircraft, Westinghouse, Iran Electronics Industries (IEI) (1975)	Maintaining electro-optical systems on Maverick-TOW missiles. Planned production (under license) of subcomponents, missile assembly (2,000 TOW; 5,000 Maverick), and maintenance of tank fire-control systems, laser range-finders, and next-generation ATW (Hellfire). $300 million; training, $25 million.	Shiraz
2. Emerson/IEI (1971)	Repair and maintenance of TOW launching system, under license.	Shiraz
3. Irano-British Dynamics (British Aircraft Corporation/IEI) (1976)	Development and planned assembly of 2,500 Rapier tracked low-level anti-aircraft missiles, under license. The licensing firms mentioned in this table are U.S. corporations unless otherwise noted. App. $100 million.	Teheran (Parchin)
4. Raytheon/Imperial Iranian Air Force (IIAF)	I-Hawk surface to air missiles maintenance and repair.	Shiraz (Doshan Tappeh)

(cont'd.)

Appendix 2 (cont'd.)

	Activity	Location
5. Westinghouse/Military Industries Organization (MIO)	Sparrow and Sidewinder, maintenance and repair.	Teheran
Aircraft:		
6. Bell Helicopter-Bell Operations,[a] Iran Helicopter Industries (IHI) (1976)	Coproduce (assemble) 214A tactical transport helicopters (planned) and 214ST (new model hot day, high-altitude aircraft). Estimated cost—$125 million to $400 million.	Esfahan
7. Bell Helicopter International/Imperial Iranian Army Aviation Branch	Turnkey operation to overhaul and provide logistics for 214A, 214B, and 202AH-IJ helicopters. Training component: $225 million.	Esfahan
8. Northrop/Iran Aircraft Industries (1970)	Maintenance and modification of Iranian military and civilian planes. Planned licensed production of parts and aircraft assembly (49% Northrop, 51% Iranian government).	Teheran, Esfahan, Bushehr, Shiraz, Tabriz
9. Hawker (British), Shahbaz	Planned Audax aircraft maintenance and repair.	Shiraz (Doshan Tappeh)
10. Grumman-General Devices/Grumman Iran Private Co., Ltd.	F-14 maintenance.	Esfahan

(cont'd.)

159

Appendix 2 (cont'd.)

	Activity	Location
11. Lockheed Aircraft Service Co./IACI General Electric/IACI	Expansion of aircraft overhaul and maintenance facilities. PEACELOG contract to design and equip engine shops. $128 million.	Teheran
12. Western Electric/Imperial Iranian Air Force (IIAF)	Repairing electronic systems on McDonnell-Douglas F-4s.	Teheran
13. Agusta-Elicotteri-Meridionali (Italy) IHI (1974)	Maintenance, repair, spare parts for Chinook. Planned assembly ($100 million).	Teheran
Armored vehicles and ordnance:		
14. Irano-British Dynamics (Vickers)	Chieftain tank repair (planned).	Shiraz
15. Bowen-McLaughlin (US)	M-47 retrofitting.	Masjed Soleyman
16. Fritz Werner[b] (FRG); Heckler, Koch, Rheinmetall (FRG)	Small arms, ammunition, tank chains, repair, under license (export to Asia and Africa planned).	Teheran (Parchin)
17. Munich Motor and Turbine (MTO) Daimler-Benz (MAN) (1974)	Various military vehicles.	undetermined
18. Bofors (Sweden)	Explosives and antitank missiles manufacture.	Teheran, planned Esfahan complex

(cont'd.)

(cont'd.)

Appendix 2 (cont'd.)

	Activity	Location
19. Millbank Technical Services (UK),c Wimpey-Laing (UK)/MIO	Construction of ordnance complex for tank ammunition, parts, and production (planned). ($1,275, projected cost)	Esfahan
Communications and support:		
20. Messerschmitt-Boelkow-Blohm (FRG)/ Iran Advanced Technology Corp.	Software, electronics technology, systems design, space and aeronautics development.	Teheran
21. Honeywell (US)/ISIRAN (app. 1975)	Maintenance, repair, military computer systems.	
22. Iran Telecommunications Company (Siemens [FRG]/Ministry of War)	Radio handsets.	Shiraz
23. Page (Northrop)d/Ministry of War (1972), American Bell International (USA, 1975)	Installation of integrated telecommunications system including military. Total cost of telecommunications projects: $14 billion over 10-year period including civilian.	Teheran

Appendix 2 (cont'd.)

Activity

24. GTE/IEI (1975)

Supply electronic switching equipment for telecommunications and manufacture switches (plant was never established). Part of Bell contract. Messerschmitt held 35 percent of the shares in IATG (Iran Advanced Technology Corporation); the remainder were held by the National Iranian Oil Company, Industrial Development and Reconstruction Organization, Bank Omran, and the air force's University of Science and Technology.

25. Control Data (USA)/Computer Terminals of Iran

Research and production under license, military applications (70% Iranian government, 30% control data).

---

[a]General Electric also involved with engines, electronics, hydraulics, and special materials.
[b]Small arms were produced under license from Heckler and Koch (a government-owned company), and Rheinmetall.
[c]Millbank is British government-owned. Its contract apparently encompassed agreements relating to tank repair production with Wimpey-Laing and Vickers (Chieftains).
[d]Head of four-country international consortium.

162

Bibliography

MILITARY SECURITY AND MILITARY EXPENDITURES

Abrahamian, Ervand. *Iran Between Two Revolutions.* Princeton: Princeton University Press, 1982.
Adekanye, J. Bayo. *The Role of Military Expenditures in Nigerian Development.* University of Ibadan, 1983. Mimeo.
Agarwal, Rajesh K. *Defense Production and Development.* New Delhi: Arnold-Heineman, 1978.
Albrecht, Ulrich. "Arming the Developing Countries." *International Social Science Journal* 28, 2 (1976): 326-340.
—. "Militarized Sub-Imperialism: Iran." In Mary Kaldor and Asbjorn Eide, eds., *The World Military Order: The Impact of Military Technology on the Third World.* London: Macmillan, 1979; New York: Praeger, 1979, pp. 137-179.
Amirsadeghi, Hossein, ed. *The Security of the Persian Gulf.* New York: St. Martin's Press, 1981.
—. *Twentieth Century Iran.* London: Heinemann, 1977.
Askari, Hossein and Vittorio Gorbo. "Economic Implications of Military Expenditures in the Middle East." *Journal of Peace Research* 2 (1974): 341-343.
Ball, Nicole. "Defense and Development: A Critique of the Benoit Study." *Economic Development and Cultural Change* 31 (April 1983): 507-524.
—. "Defense Expenditures and Economic Growth: A Comment." *Armed Forces and Society* 11, 2 (Winter 1985): 291-297.

—. "Measuring Third World Security Expenditure: A Research Note." *World Development* 12, 2 (February 1984): 157-164.

—. *The Military in the Development Process: A Guide to Issues.* Claremont, Calif.: Regina Books, 1981.

—. "Military Expenditure and Socio-economic Development." *International Social Science Journal* 35, 1 (1983): 81-97.

—. *Security and Economy in the Third World: The Role of Security Expenditure in the Development Process.* Princeton: Princeton University Press, 1989.)

—. "Security Expenditure and Economic Growth in Developing Countries." Paper presented at the East-West Conference on North-South Relations, Frankfurt, March 22, 1985.

Ball, Nicole and Milton Leitenberg. "Disarmament and Development: Their Interrelationship." Paper prepared for the RIO.

—, eds. *The Structure of the Defense Industry: An International Survey.* New York: St. Martin's Press, 1983.

—. *Third World Security Expenditure: A Statistical Compendium.* FOA Report. Stockholm: National Defense Research Agency, 1984.

Barnaby, Frank and Ron Huisken. *Arms Uncontrolled.* Cambridge: Harvard University Press, 1975.

Bayne, E.A. and R.O. Collin. "Arms and Advisors: Views From Saudi Arabia and Iran." American Universities Field Staff, *Southwest Asia Series* 19 (1976).

Benoit, Emile. *Defense and Economic Growth in Developing Countries.* Lexington, Mass.: Lexington Books, 1973.

Berman, Robert P. "The Shah's Iranian Empire: Old Games, New Stakes (Ours)." In *The Persian Gulf, 1974: Money, Politics, Arms, and Power.* Hearings Before the Subcommittee on the Near East and South Asia, Committee on Foreign Affairs, U.S. House of Representatives, July 1974.

Bienen, Henry. "Armed Forces and National Modernization: Continuing the Debate." *Comparative Politics* 17, 1 (October 1982): 41-60.

Bolton, R.E. *Defense Purchases and Regional Growth.* Washington, D.C.: Brookings Institution, 1966.

Brzoska, Michael. "Arms Transfer Data Sources." *Journal of Conflict Resolution* 26, 1 (March 1982): 50-65.

—. *External Trade, Indebtedness, Foreign Direct Investment and the Military Sector in LDCs: A Study of the Effects of Militarization on External Eco-*

nomic Relations. Hamburg: Working Group on Armament and Underdevelopment, IFSH, November 1982. Mimeo.

—. "The Reporting of Military Expenditures." *Journal of Peace Research* 18, 3 (1981): 261-275.

Burt, R.R. *Development in Arms Transfers: Implications for Supplies and Recipient Autonomy.* Santa Monica, Calif.: Rand Corporation, 1977.

Cahn, Anne Hessing. "Determinants of the Nuclear Option: The Case of Iran." In Onkar Marwah and Ann Schulz, eds., *Nuclear Proliferation and the Near-Nuclear Countries.* Cambridge, Mass.: Ballinger, 1975.

Cahn, Anne Hessing et al. *Controlling Future Arms Trade.* New York: McGraw-Hill, 1977.

Canby, Steven L. "The Iranian Military: Political Symbolism Versus Military Usefulness." In Hossein Amirsadeghi, ed., *The Security of the Persian Gulf.* New York: St. Martin's Press, 1981; pp. 100-130.

Carr, C.D. "The United States-Iranian Relationship 1948-1978: A Study in Reverse Influence." In Hossein Amirsadeghi, ed., *The Security of the Persian Gulf,* pp. 57-84.

Carranza, Mario Estaban. "The Role of Military Expenditure in the Development Process: The Argentina Case 1946-1980." *Ibero-Americana* 12, 1-2 (1983).

Chubin, Shahram. "Implications of the Military Buildup in Less Industrial States." In Uri Ra'anan et al., eds., *Arms Transfers to the Third World: The Military Buildup in Less Industrial Countries.* Boulder, Col.: Westview Press, 1978, pp. 257-280.

—. "The International Politics of the Persian Gulf." *British Journal of International Studies* 2, 3 (October 1976).

—. "Iran Between the Arab East and the Asian West." *Survival* (July-August 1974): 180-181.

—. "Iran's Foreign Policy 1960-1976: An Overview." In Hossein Amirsadeghi, ed., *Twentieth Century Iran.* New York: Holmes & Meier, 1977.

Chubin, Shahram and Sepehr Zabih. *The Foreign Relations of Iran.* Berkeley: University of California Press, 1974.

Cottrell, Alvin J. "Iran's Armed Forces Under the Pahlavi Dynasty." In George Lenczowski, ed., *Iran Under the Pahlavis.* Stanford, Calif.: Hoover Institution Press, 1978, pp. 389-432.

Cottrell, Alvin J. and Frank Bray. *Military Forces in the Persian Gulf.* Washington Papers 6. Washington, D.C.: Center for Strategic and International Studies, Georgetown University, 1978.

Crouch, Harold. "Generals and Business in Indonesia." *Pacific Affairs* 48 (Winter 1975/76): 519-540.

Deger, Saadet. "The Developmental Effect of Military Expenditure in LDCs." Paper prepared for Colloque on Armement-Developpment-Droits de l'Homme-Desarmement, October 29, 1982. London: University of London.

——. *Military Expenditure in Third World Countries: The Economic Effects.* International Library of Economics series. London: Routledge & Kegan Paul, 1986.

Deger, Saadet and Ron Smith. "Military Expenditure and Growth in Less Developed Countries." *Journal of Conflict Resolution* 27, 2 (June 1983): 335-363.

Dessouki, Ali E. and Abdel al-Labban. "Arms Race, Defense Expenditures and Development: The Egyptian Case 1952-1973." *Journal of South Asian and Middle Eastern Studies* 4, 3 (Spring 1981): 65-71.

Dillingham, L.D. et al. *Iranian Arms Acquisition and the Politics of Cooperative Regionalism.* Research Report 40. Wright Patterson Air Force Base, Ohio: Air Force Institute of Technology, August 1975. AD-A016-8391.

Economist Intelligence Unit. *The Economic Effects of Disarmament.* London: EIU, 1963.

Ehrenberg, Eckehart. "Rustung und Wirtschaft am Golf: Der Teran und Seine Nachbarn." In *DGKK-PP, Papiere fur di Praxis* 11. Bonn, 1979.

Eide, Asbjorn. "The Transfer of Arms to Third World Countries and Their Internal Uses." *International Social Science Journal* 28, 2 (1976): 307-325.

Encinas del Pando, Jose. *Economic, Military, and Socio-Political Variables in Argentina, Chile, and Peru.* Lima: University of Lima, 1983. Mimeo.

——. "The Role of Military Expenditure in the Development Process: Peru—. A Case Study, 1950-1980." *Nordic Journal of Latin American Studies* 12, 1-2 (1983): 51-114.

Faini, R., P. Annez and L. Taylor. "Defense Spending, Economic Structure, and Growth: Evidence Among Countries and Over Time." *Economic Development and Cultural Change* 32, 3 (April 1984): 487-498.

Fesharaki, Fereidun. "Revolution and Energy Policy in Iran: International and Domestic Implications." In H. Amirsadeghi, ed., *The Security of the Persian Gulf.* New York: St. Martin's Press, 1981.

Franko, Patrice. "Swords Into Plowshares: Demilitarizing Development

Strategies." *New Catholic World* 226 (March-April 1982): 74-77.

Frederiksen, P.C. and Robert E. Looney. "Defense Expenditures and Economic Growth in Developing Countries." *Armed Forces and Society* 9, 4 (Summer 1983): 633-645.

Furlong, R.D.M. "Iran: A Power to Be Reckoned With." *International Defense Review* (June 1973).

Galbraith, John K. *The New Industrial State.* Boston: Houghton-Mifflin, 1971.

Gates, Gregory Francis. *An Analysis of the Impact of American Arms Transfers on Political Stability in Iran.* National Technical Information Service. September 1980. AD-A093 255.

Ghosh, Pradip K., ed. *Disarmament and Development: A Global Perspective.* Westport, Conn.: Greenwood Press, 1984.

Gootheil, Fred M. "An Economic Assessment of the Military Burden in the Middle East: 1960-1980." *Journal of Conflict Resolution* 12, 2 (September 1974): 502-513.

Graham, Thomas. "India's Military Industrial Research Complex." Paper presented at the conference of the International Studies Association, Cincinnati, March 25, 1982.

Griffith, William E. "Iran's Foreign Policy in the Pahlavi Era." In George Lenczowski, ed., *Iran Under the Pahlavis.* Stanford, Calif.: Hoover Institution Press, 1978, pp. 365-388.

Haftendorn, Helga. *Militärhilfe und Rüstungsexporte der BRD.* Dusseldorf: Bertelsmann Universitats Verlag, 1971.

Hamon, Leo, ed. *Le Role Extra-Militaire de l'Armee Dans Le Tiers Monde.* Paris: Centre d'Etudes des Relations Politiques, Universite de Dijon, 1966.

Harkavy, Robert E. *The Arms Trade and the International System.* Cambridge, Mass.: Ballinger, 1975.

Helper, Susan. "Military Spending and Growth in Developing Countries: A Review of Some Econometric Evidence." Paper presented at the Conference on Development and Security in the Third World, Fletcher School of Law and Diplomacy, Tufts University, April 12-13, 1984.

Heshmati, Manouchehri. "Die Rolle des Militars in der Unterentwickelten Gesellschaft-auf Beispiel Persiens." Berlin, 1974. Mimeo.

Hickman, William F. "How the Iranian Military Expelled the Iraqis."

Brookings Review 1, 3 (Spring 1983): 19-23.

Hoffman, Stanley. "Security in an Age of Turbulence: Means of Response." In Christoph Bertram, ed., *Third-World Conflict and International Security.* London: International Institute for Strategic Studies, 1981.

Horowitz, Irving Louis. *Beyond Empire and Revolution: Militarization and Consolidation in the Third World.* New York: Oxford University Press, 1982.

Huisken, Ron. "Armaments and Development." In Helena Tuomi and Raimo Vayrynen, eds., *Militarization and Arms Production.* London: Croom Helm, 1983.

Hunter, Robert. "Arms Control in the Persian Gulf." In Andrew J. Pierre, ed., *Arms Transfers and American Foreign Policy.* New York: New York University Press, 1979.

"Indian Defense Forces and Arms Production." *Bulletin of Concerned Asian Scholars* 13, 1 (n.d., app. 1980).

The Iranian Military Under the Islamic Republic. Santa Monica, Calif.: Rand Corporation, n.d.

Janowitz, Morris. *Sociology and the Military Establishment.* 3rd ed. Beverly Hills, Calif.: Sage Publications, 1974.

Jencks, Harlan W. "The Chinese 'Military-Industrial' Complex and Defense Modernization." *Asian Survey* 20, 10 (October 1980): 965-989.

Johnson, John J., ed. *The Role of the Military in Underdeveloped Countries.* Princeton: Princeton University Press, 1962.

Jolly, Richard, ed. *Disarmament and World Development.* Oxford: Pergamon Press, 1978.

Jones, Rodney and Steven A. Hildreth. *Modern Weapons and Third World Powers.* CSIS Significant Issues Series 6, 4. Boulder, Col.: Westview Press, 1984.

Jong-Chun, Baek. "The Role of the Republic of Korea Armed Forces in National Development: Past and Future." *Journal of East Asian Affairs* 3, 2 (Fall/Winter 1983): 292-323.

Kaldor, Mary. "The Military in Development." *World Development* 4, 6 (1976): 459-482.

Kemp, Geoffrey. "Arms Transfers and the 'Back-End' Problems in Developing Countries." In Stephanie Neuman and Robert Harkavy, eds., *Arms Transfers in the Modern World.* New York: Praeger, 1980, pp. 294-314.

—. "Classification of Weapons Systems and Force Designs in Less Developed Country Environments: Implications for Arms Transfer Policies." Cambridge, Mass.: Center for International Studies, Massachusetts Institute of Technology, 1970.

Kennedy, Edward. "The Persian Gulf: Arms Race or Arms Control." *Foreign Affairs* 54, 1 (October 1975): 14-35.

Khomeyni, Ayatollah Ruhollah. *Islamic Government.* n.p., n.d.

Klare, Michael T. "America's White-Collar Mercenaries." *Inquiry* 16 (October 1978).

—. *Supplying Repression: U.S. Support for Authoritarian Regimes.* Washington D.C.: Institute for Policy Studies, 1977.

Kodzic, Peter. "Armaments and Development." In David Carlton and C. Shaeffers, eds., *The Dynamics of the Arms Race.* New York: Wiley, 1975.

Kolodziej, Edward A. "Measuring French Arms Transfers: A Problem of Sources and Some Sources of Problems With ACDA Data." *Journal of Conflict Resolution* 23, 2 (June 1979): 195-227.

Kolodziej, Edward A. and Robert Harkavy, eds. *Security Policies of Developing Countries.* Lexington, Mass.: Lexington Books, 1982.

Korea University, Labor Education and Research Institute. *Economic Development and Military Technical Manpower of Korea: A Study of Manpower Development in the Military of Korea.* Seoul: Korea University Press, 1976.

Korn, Chakrit Noranitpadung. "Thailand's National Economic Development Corporation Limited: An Evaluation With Special Emphasis on the Political Implications." *Thai Journal of Development Administration* 9 (October 1969): 732-745.

Ladjevardi, Habib. "The Origins of U.S. Support for an Autocratic Iran." *International Journal of Middle East Studies* 15 (1983): 225-239.

Leiss, Amelia C. "Changing Patterns of Arms Transfers: Implications for Arms Transfers Policies." Cambridge, Mass.: Center for International Studies, Massachusetts Institute of Technology, 1970.

Leitenberg, Milton. "Notes on the Diversion of Resources for Military Purposes in Developing Nations." *Journal of Peace Research* 2 (1976): 111-116.

Leitenberg, Milton and Nicole Ball. "The Military Expenditure of Less Developed Nations as a Proportion of Their State Budgets." *Bulletin of Peace Proposals* 8, 4 (1974).

Leontief, Wassily and Faye Duchin. *Military Spending: Facts and Figures, World-wide Implications and Future Outlook.* New York: Oxford University Press, 1983.

—. "World-wide Implications of Hypothetical Changes in Military Spending: An Input-Output Approach." New York: Institute for Economic Analysis, New York University, 1980.

Lissack, M. "Social Change, Mobilization, and the Exchange of Services Between the Military Establishment and Civil Society." *Economic Development and Cultural Change* 13 (1964).

Litwak, Robert. *Security in the Persian Gulf.* Vol. 2. *Sources of Interstate Conflict.* London: International Institute for Strategic Studies, 1981.

Lock, Peter and Herbert Wulf. "The Economic Consequences of the Transfer of Military-Oriented Technology." In Mary Kaldor and Asbjorn Eide, eds., *The World Military Order: The Impact of Military Technology on the Third World.* London: Macmillan, 1979; New York: Praeger, 1979.

—. *Register of Arms Production in Developing Countries.* Hamburg: University of Hamburg, Study Group in Armaments and Underdevelopment, 1977.

Marwah, Onkar. "India's Military Power and Policy." In Onkar Marwah and Jonathan Pollack, eds., *Military Power in Asian States.* Boulder, Col.: Westview Press, 1980.

McNaugher, Thomas L. "Arms and Allies on the Arabian Peninsula." *Orbis* (Fall 1984): 489-526.

Mehta, Jagat S. *Third World Militarization.* Austin: University of Texas Press, 1984, p. 54.

Melman, Seymour. *The Permanent War Economy: American Capitalism in Decline.* New York: Simon & Schuster, 1974.

Moodie, Michael. "Defense Industries in the Third World: Problems and Promises." In Stephanie B. Neuman and Robert E. Harkavy, eds., *Arms Transfers in the Modern World.* New York: Praeger, 1980.

Moran, Theodore H. "Iranian Defense Expenditures and the Social Crisis." *International Security* 3, 3 (Winter 1978/79): 178-192.

Naur, M. "Industrialization and Transfer of Civil and Military Technology to the Arab Countries." *Current Research on Peace and Violence* 3, 3-4 (1980): 153-176.

Neuman, Stephanie G. *Into the Crystal Ball: Third World Military Industries—. Implications for the Global Arms Transfer System and U.S. Na-*

tional Security Interests. Washington, D.C.: Department of State, Office of Long-Range Assessments and Research, 1973.

—. "Security, Military Expenditures and Socioeconomic Development: Reflections on Iran." *Orbis* 22, 3 (Fall 1978): 569-594.

—. *Unravelling the Triad: Arms Transfers, Indigenous Defense Production, and Dependency—. Iran as an Example.* Washington, D.C.: Department of State, Foreign Affairs Research Documentation Center, 1979.

Parvin, Manoucher. "Military Expenditure in Iran: A Forgotten Question." *Iranian Studies* 1 (Fall 1968): 149-154.

Pfau, Richard. "The Legal Status of American Forces in Iran." *Middle East Journal* 28, 2 (1974): 141-153.

Pierre, Andrew J. *The Global Politics of Arms Sales.* Princeton: Princeton University Press, 1982.

Portales, Carlos. "The Role of Military Expenditures in the Development Process: Case of Chile, 1952-1973 and 1973-1980—Two Contrasting Cases." *Ibero-Americana, Nordic Journal of Latin American Studies* 12, 1-2 (1983): 21-50.

Price, D.F. *Oman: Insurgency and Development.* London: Institute for the Study of Conflict, 1975.

Pryor, Leslie M. (psued.). "Arms and the Shah." *Foreign Policy* 31 (Summer 1978): 56-71.

Pye, Lucien W. "Arms in the Process of Political Modernization." In John J. Johnson, ed., *The Role of the Military in Underdeveloped Countries.* Princeton: Princeton University Press, 1962.

Qadimi, Zabibollah Rezlami. *Tarikh-e Bist-o-Panj Sal-e Artesh Shahanshahiye Iran* (Twenty-Five-Year History of the Imperial Army of Iran). Teheran: Majles & Nate Bank, 1945.

Ra'anan, Uri, Robert L. Pfaltzgraff, Jr. and Geoffrey Kemp. *Arms Transfers to the Third World: The Military Buildup in Less Industrial Countries.* Boulder, Col.: Westview Press, 1978.

Ramazani, Rouhollah K. *Iran's Foreign Policy 1941-1973.* Charlottesville, Va.: University Press of Virginia, 1975.

Rieffel, Alexis and Aminda S. Wirjasuptra. "Military Enterprises." *Bulletin of Indonesian Economic Studies* (July 1972): 104-109.

Rosen, Steven J. "The Proliferation of New Land-Based Technologies: Implications for Local Military Balances." In Stephanie B. Neuman and Robert E. Harkavy, eds., *Arms Transfers in the Modern World.* New York: Praeger, 1980.

—. *Testing the Theory of the Military and Industrial Complex.* Lexington, Mass.: Lexington Books, 1973.

Rothschild, K.W. "Military Expenditure, Exports, and Growth." *Kyklos* 26, 4 (1973): 804-814.

Rothstein, Robert L. *The Weak in the World of the Strong: The Developing Countries in the International System.* New York: Columbia University Press, 1977.

Sampson, Anthony. *The Arms Bazaar: From Lebanon to Lockheed.* New York: Viking Press, 1977.

Schahgaldian, N. and G. Barkhordian. *The Iranian Military Under the Islamic Republic.* Santa Monica, Calif.: Rand Corporation, March 1987.

Schultze, Charles L. "Economic Effects of the Defense Budget." *Brookings* 18, 2 (Fall 1981): 1-5.

Schulz, Ann. "Iran: A Second Order Power Turns Revolutionary." In Edward A. Kolodziej and Robert E. Harkavy, eds., *Security Policies of Emerging States: A Comparative Approach.* Lexington, Mass.: Lexington Books, 1982.

—. "Iran : State-Building and the Defense Community." Paper delivered to the Section on Military Studies, International Studies Association, Kiawah Island, South Carolina, November 1978.

Sivard, Ruth L. "Let Them Eat Bullets: A Statistical Portrait of World Militarism." *Bulletin of Atomic Scientists* (April 1975).

—. *World Military and Social Expenditures.* Leesburg, Va.: World Priorities. Various years.

Stanhope, Henry. "Iran's Defense Budget." *Defense Journal* 2 (April/May 1976).

Stockholm International Peace Research Institute. *World Armaments and Disarmament, SIPRI Yearbook.* London: Taylor & Francis; previously, Stockholm: Almquist & Wiksell, various years.

Subrahmanyam, K. *Defense and Development.* Calcutta: Minerva, 1973.

Taheri, Amir. "Policies of Iran in the Persian Gulf Region." In Abbas Amirie, ed., *The Persian Gulf and the Indian Ocean in International Politics.* Teheran: Institute for International Political and Economic Studies, 1975.

Tahtinen, Dale R. *Arms in the Persian Gulf.* Washington, D.C.: American Enterprise Institute, 1974.

Tapar, R. "State of the Military." *The Statesman Weekly,* September 19, 1981.

Taylor, Lance. "The Costly Arms Trade." *New York Times*, December 22, 1981.

Terhal, P. "Guns or Grain: Macro-Economic Costs of Indian Defense, 1969-70." *Economic and Political Weekly* (Bombay) 16, 49 (December 5, 1981): 1995-2004.

Toumi, Helena and Raimo Vayrynan. *Transnational Corporations, Armaments, and Development.* New York: St. Martin's Press, 1982.

U.N. Department for Disarmament Affairs. *Economic and Social Consequences of the Arms Race and of Military Expenditures.* Report of the Secretary General. New York: United Nations, 1983.

U.N. Department of Political and Security Council Affairs. *Reduction of Military Budgets; Measurement and International Reporting of Military Expenditures: Report Prepared by the Group of Experts on the Reduction of Military Budgets.* New York: United Nations, 1977.

U.N. General Assembly. *Study on the Relationship Between Disarmament and Development.* Report of the Secretary General. New York: United Nations, 1981.

U.S. Agency for International Development. *Economic Development Versus Military Expenditures in Countries Receiving U.S. Aid: Priorities and Competition for Resources.* Report submitted to the Committees on Foreign Affairs and Foreign Relations. Washington, D.C.: U.S. Government Printing Office, 1980.

U.S. Arms Control and Disarmament Agency. *The International Transfer of Conventional Arms.* A Report to Congress from the Arms Control and Disarmament Association. Washington, D.C.: U.S. Government Printing Office, 1971.

—. *World Military Expenditures and Arms Transfers.* Washington, D.C.: USACDA, various years.

U.S. Central Intelligence Agency. *Handbook of Economic Statistics, 1980.* Washington, D.C.: CIA, 1980.

U.S. Commission on Security and Economic Assistance. *A Report to the Secretary of State.* Washington, D.C.: The Commission, 1983.

U.S. Comptroller General's Office. *Comptroller General's Report to the Congress 1975: Issues Related to U.S. Military Sales and Assistance to Iran.* Washington, D.C.: U.S. Government Printing Office, 1975.

U.S. Department of Defense. *Military Assistance and FMS Facts* (subsequently titled *Foreign Military Sales and Military Assistance Facts*). Washington, D.C.: U.S. Government Printing Office, various years.

U.S. Department of State. *Security Assistance Programs FY1981.* Presentation to Congress. Washington, D.C.: The Department, 1981.

U.S. Export-Import Bank. *Annual Report.* Washington, D.C.: The Bank, 1969.

U.S. House of Representatives, Committee on International Relations. *New Perspectives on the Persian Gulf.* Hearings Before the Subcommittee on the Near East and South Asia, 1973. Washington, D.C.: U.S. Government Printing Office, 1974.

—. *The Persian Gulf, 1974: Money, Politics, Arms and Power.* Hearings Before the Subcommittee on the Near East and South Asia, 1974. Washington, D.C.: U.S. Government Printing Office, 1975.

—. *The Persian Gulf, 1975: The Continuing Debate on Arms Sales.* Hearings Before a Special Subcommittee on Investigations. Washington, D.C.: U.S. Government Printing Office, 1975.

—. *United States Arms Policies in the Persian Gulf and Red Sea Areas: Past, Present, and Future.* Report of a Staff Survey Mission to Ethiopia, Iran, and the Arabian Peninsula, December 1977. Washington, D.C.: U.S. Government Printing Office, 1976.

—. *United States Arms Sales to the Persian Gulf: Report on a Study Mission to Iran, Kuwait, and Saudi Arabia, 1975.* Washington, D.C.: U.S. Government Printing Office, 1976.

—. *United States Interests in and Policies Toward the Persian Gulf.* Hearings Before the Subcommittee on the Near East and South Asia, 1972. Washington, D.C.: U.S. Government Printing Office, 1973.

U.S. Senate, Committee on Foreign Relations. *U.S. Military Sales to Iran: A Staff Report to the Subcommittee on Foreign Assistance.* Washington, D.C.: U.S. Government Printing Office, 1976.

Vagts, Alfred. *History of Militarism.* New York: Meridian Books, 1979.

Vengroff, Richard. "Soldiers and Civilians in the Third Republic." *Africa Report* 25 (January/February 1980): 7-8.

Wallensteen, Peter. *Global Militarization.* Boulder, Col.: Westview Press, 1984.

West, Robert L. "Provision for National Security in Developing Countries." Preparatory note for participants in the Conference on Development and Security in the Third World, Fletcher School of Law and Diplomacy, Tufts University, April 12-13, 1984. Mimeo.

Whynes, David K. *The Economics of Third World Military Expenditures.* Austin: University of Texas Press, 1979.

Wolpin, Miles D. *Militarism and Social Revolution in the Third World*. To-towa, N.J.: Allanheld, Osmun, 1981.

Wright, Claudia. "Implications of the Iraq-Iran War." *Foreign Affairs* 59, 2 (Winter 1980/81): 276-303.

POLITICS, ECONOMICS, AND HISTORY

Abrahamian, Ervand. "Oriental Despotism: The Case of Qajar Iran." *International Journal of Middle East Studies* 5, 1 (January 1974): 3-31.

Ajami, Ismail. "Agrarian Reform, Modernization of Peasants and Agricultural Development in Iran." In Jane W. Jacqz, ed., *Iran: Past, Present and Future*. New York: Aspen Institute for Humanistic Studies, 1976, pp. 131-156.

Akhavi, Shahrough. *Religion and Politics in Contemporary Iran: Clergy-State Relations in the Pahlavi Period*. Albany: State University of New York Press, 1980.

Aminzadeh, F. "Human Resources Development: Problems and Prospects." In Jane W. Jacqz, ed., *Iran: Past, Present and Future*. New York: Aspen Institute for Humanistic Studies, 1976.

Amirie, Abbas. *The Persian Gulf and Indian Ocean in International Politics*. Teheran: Institute for International Political and Economic Studies, 1975.

Amirie, Abbas and Hamilton Twitchell, eds. *Iran in the 1980s*. Teheran: Institute for International Political and Economic Studies, 1978.

Amirsadeghi, Hossein. *Twentieth Century Iran*. New York: Holmes & Meier, 1977.

Amuzegar, Jahangir and M. Ali Fekrat. *Iran: Economic Development Under Dualistic Conditions*. Chicago: University of Chicago Press, 1971.

Aresvik, Oddvar. *The Agricultural Development of Iran*. New York: Praeger, 1976.

Ashraf, Ahmad. "Historical Obstacles to the Development of a Bourgeoisie in Iran." *Iranian Studies* 2, 2-3 (Spring/Summer 1969): 54-79.

Australian Trade Commissioner. "Review of Economic and Commercial Post Activities." Memorandum. Teheran, 1978.

Avery, Peter. *Modern Iran*. New York: Praeger, 1965.

Avramovic, D. "Industrialization of Iran: The Records, the Problems and the Prospects." *Tahqiqat-e Eqtesadi* 7, 18 (Spring 1970): 14-47.

Bagley, F.R.C. "A Bright Future After Oil: Dams and Agro-Industry in Khuzistan." *Middle East Journal* 30, 1 (Winter 1976): 25-35.

—. "Technocracy in Iran." *Der Islam* 44 (July 1968): 230-249.

Bakhash, Shaul. "Center-Periphery Relations in Nineteenth Century Iran." *Iranian Studies* 14, 1-2 (Winter/Spring 1981): 29-51.

Bartsch, William H. "The Industrial Labor Force of Iran: Problems of Recruitment, Training, and Productivity." *Middle East Journal* 25, 1 (Winter 1971): 15-30.

—. *Problems of Employment Creation in Iran.* Employment Research Papers. Geneva: International Labour Office, 1970.

Bashiriyeh, Hossein. *The State and Revolution in Iran 1962-1982.* London: Croom Helm; New York: St. Martin's, 1984.

Bharier, Julian. *Economic Development in Iran 1900-1970.* New York: Oxford University Press, 1971.

—. "The Iranian Rial." *International Currency Review* (July 1970): 10-15.

Bill, James A. and Carl Leiden. *The Middle East: Politics and Power.* Boston: Allyn & Bacon, 1974.

Binder, Leonard. "Iran." In *The Political Economy of the Middle East 1973-78: A Compendium of Papers.* Submitted to the Joint Economic Committee, Congress of the United States. Washington, D.C.: U.S. Government Printing Office, 1980.

Brun, Thierry and Rene Dumont. "Iran: Imperial Pretensions and Agricultural Dependence." *Merip Reports* 8, 8 (1978): 15-20.

Carey, J.P.C. and A.G. Carey. "Industrial Growth and Development Planning in Iran." *Middle East Journal* 29, 1 (Winter 1975): 1-15.

—. "Iran's Agriculture and Its Development: 1952-1973." *International Journal of Middle East Studies* 7 (1976): 359-382.

Cline, William R. et al. *World Inflation and the Developing Countries.* Washington, D.C.: Brookings Institution, 1980.

Daftary, Farhad and Maryann Borghey. *Multinational Enterprises and Employment in Iran.* World Employment Research Working Paper. Geneva: International Labour Office, 1976. Mimeo.

Diaz-Alejandro, Carlos F. "Southern Core Stabilization Plans." In William R. Cline and Sidney Weintraub, eds., *Economic Stabilization in Developing Countries.* Washington, D.C.: Brookings Institution, 1981.

Djalili, Yassaman Saadatmand. "A Review on the Agricultural Development in Iran (from 1900 to 1981)." Paper presented at the International Development Workshop, University of New Hampshire, Durham, December 2, 1981.

Doroudian, R. "Modernization of Rural Economy in Iran." In Jane W. Jacqz, ed., *Iran: Past, Present and Future*. New York: Aspen Institute for Humanistic Studies, 1976.

Eshag, Eprime. "Study on the Excess Cost of Tied Economic Aid Given to Iran in 1966/67." *Tahqiqat-e Eqtesadi* 8, 22 (Spring 1971).

Farvar, M. Taqi et al. "The Lessons of Lorestan." *CERES* 50 (March/April 1976).

Fatahi, Nader and Stig Ericsson. *Migrationes Iranicae*. Sweden: Institute of Sociologie, University of Lund, 1976.

Goldberg, Ray A. "Iran-America Poultry, S.A." Case study, Seminar in Agribusiness. Cambridge: Harvard School of Business Administration, 1966.

Graham, Robert. *The Illusion of Power*. New York: St. Martin's Press, 1978.

Great Britain, Department of Overseas Trade. *Economic Survey of Iran* (formerly *Report on the Finance and Commerce of Persia*). London: Her Majesty's Stationery Office, 1925-1948.

Gupta, Raj Narain. *Iran: An Economic Study*. New Delhi: Indian Institute of International Affairs, 1947.

Hakimian, Hassan. "Iran: Dependency and Industrialization." Sussex Institute of Development Studies *Bulletin* 12, 1 (1980): 24-28.

Halliday, Fred. *Iran: Dictatorship and Development*. New York: Penguin Books, 1979.

Haqiqat, Chapour. *Iran: La Revolution Inachevee et l'Ordre American*. Paris: Editions Anthropos, 1980.

Hetherington, Norris S. "Industrialization and Revolution in Iran: Force Progress or Unmet Expectation?" *Middle East Journal* 36, 3 (Summer 1982): 362-373.

Hirsch, Etienne. *Employment and Income Policies for Iran*. Geneva: International Labour Office, 1973.

Iran, Bank Markazi. *Annual Report and Balance Sheet*. Teheran: Bank, 1963-1972.

—. *National Income of Iran 1959-1972*. Teheran: Bureau of National Accounts, 1974.

Iran, Ministry of Economy. *Report on the Results of Annual Industrial Survey in 1964*. Teheran: Ministry of Economy, 1964.

Iran, Ministry of Labor. *National Manpower Resources and Requirements Sur-*

vey, Iran 1959. Teheran: Eslamyeh, 1959.

Iran, Plan and Budget Organization. *Budget Act for the Entire Country*. Teheran: Organization, various years.

—. *Fourth National Development Plan 1968-1972*. Teheran: Organization, 1968.

—. *Iran's Fifth Development Plan 1973-1978*. Teheran: Organization, 1973.

—. *Outline of the Third Plan 1341-1346 (1962-1967)*. Teheran: Organization, 1965.

—. *Sixth Plan Policy Questions*. Teheran: Organization, Planning Division, Planometrics and General Economy Bureau, 1976.

Iran, Plan and Budget Organization, Statistical Centre of Iran. *The Results of the 1972 Census of Large Industrial Establishments*. Teheran: Statistical Centre, 1973.

—. *Statistical Yearbook of Iran*. Teheran: Statistical Centre, 1967, 1976.

Issawi, Charles. "The Iranian Economy 1925-1975: Fifty Years of Economic Development." In George Lenczowski, ed., *Iran Under the Pahlavis*. Stanford, Calif.: Hoover Institution Press, 1978.

Johnson, Gail Cook. *High-Level Manpower in Iran*. New York: Praeger, 1980.

Katouzian, Homa. *The Political Economy of Modern Iraq: Despotism and Pseudo-Modernism*. New York: New York University Press, 1980.

Kavoosi, Rostam M. "The Industrial Exports of Iran." Working paper. Teheran: Iran Planning Institute, 1978.

—. "Structural Change in the Iranian Manufacturing Industry, 1959-1972." Unpublished doctoral dissertation, Harvard University, 1976.

Kedourie, Elie and Sylvia G. Haim, eds. *Towards a Modern Iran: Studies in Thought, Politics and Society*. London: Frank Cass, 1980.

Klein, D. "Fiscal and Credit Policies." Employment and Income Policies for Iran, Mission Working Paper 10. Geneva: International Labour Office, 1973.

Kooros, Ahmad. "Economic Growth and Labor Participation in Iran: A Rejoinder." *Tahqiqat-e Eqtesadi* 7, 18 (Spring 1970): 90-91.

Korby, Wilfried. *Probleme der Industriellen Entwicklung und Konzentration in Iran*. Beihafte zum Tubinger Atlas des Vorderen Orients 13, 20. Wiesbaden: Dr. Ludwig Reicher Verlag, 1977.

Kurtzig, Michael. "U.S. Farm Sales to Iran Have Headed Downward."

Foreign Agriculture 14, 21 (May 24, 1976): 4.

Looney, Robert E. *A Development Strategy for Iran Through the 1980s.* New York: Praeger, 1977.

—. *Income Distribution Policies and Economic Growth in Semi-Industrialized Countries: A Comparative Study of Iran, Mexico, Brazil, and South Korea.* New York: Praeger, 1975.

Looney, Robert E. and P.C. Frederiksen. "Defense Expenditures and Post-Revolutionary Iranian Economic Growth." *Armed Forces and Society* 9, 4 (Summer 1983): 633-646.

Lovbrock, Asbjorn. *State Interventionism, Industrial Growth and Planning in Iran.* Unpublished master's thesis, University of Oslo, 1977.

Mehner, Harold. "Development and Planning in Iran After World War II." In George Lenczowski, ed., *Iran Under the Pahlavis.* Stanford, Calif.: Hoover Institution Press, 1978, pp. 167-200.

Miklos, Jack C. *The Iranian Revolution and Modernization: Way Stations to Anarchy.* National Security Essay Series 83-2. Washington, D.C.: National Defense University Press, 1983.

Moghtader, Hushang. "The Impact of Increased Oil Revenue on Iran's Economic Development (1973-1976)." In Elie Kedourie and Sylvia G. Haim, eds., *Towards a Modern Iran: Studies in Thought, Politics and Society.* London: Frank Cass, 1980.

Motamen, Homa. *Expenditures of Oil Revenue.* New York: St. Martin's Press, 1979.

Najmabadi, F. "Strategies of Industrial Development in Iran." In Jane W. Jacqz, ed., *Iran: Past, Present and Future.* New York: Aspen Institute for Humanistic Studies, 1976.

Nowshirvani, Vahid F. "Direct Foreign Investment in the Non-Oil Sectors of the Iranian Economy." *Iranian Studies* 6, 1-3 (Spring/Summer 1973): 66-110.

Nyrop, Richard F., ed. *Iran: A Country Study.* Area Handbook Series. Washington, D.C.: U.S. Government Printing Office, 1978.

Okazaki, Shoko. *The Development of Large-Scale Farming in Iran: The Case of the Province of Gorgan.* Occasional Papers 3. Tokyo: Institute of Asian Economic Affairs, 1968.

Parvin, Manoucher and Amir N. Zamani. "Political Economy of Growth and Destruction: A Statistical Interpretation of the Iran Case." *Iranian Studies* 12, 1-2 (1979): 43-79.

Parvizi, Ali. "Report to the Ministry of Agriculture, 1972." Teheran, n.d.

Mimeo.

Payer, Cheryl. *The Debt Trap*. New York: Monthly Review Press, 1974.

Razavi, Hossein and Firouz Vakil. *The Political Environment of Economic Planning in Iran 1971-1983*. Boulder, Col.: Westview Press, 1984.

Rothschild, Emma. "Banks: The Coming Crisis." *New York Review of Books*, May 27, 1976.

—. "Banks: The Politics of Debt." *New York Review of Books*, June 24, 1976.

Rouhani, Mansur. *Towse'e eqtesadi dar qotbharje manabe'-ye ab va khak (Economic Development at the Poles of Soil and Water)*. Teheran: Ministry of Agriculture, 1967.

Rubin, Barry. *Paved With Good Intentions*. Oxford: Oxford University Press, 1980.

Rudner, Martin. "Higher Education and the Development of Science in Islamic Countries: A Comparative Analysis." *Canadian Journal of Development Studies* 4, 1 (1983): 63-94.

Sadigh, Firouz. *Impact of Government Policies on the Structure and Growth of Iranian Industry 1960-1972*. London: University of London, Faculty of Economics, 1975.

Sa'edlu, Hushang. "A Critique of 'A Policy for Agricultural Development at the Poles of Soil and Water.'" *Tahqiqat-e Eqtesadi* 9, 25/26 (Winter/Spring 1972): 54-80.

Saikal, Amin. *The Rise and Fall of the Shah*. Princeton: Princeton University Press, 1980.

Schulz, Ann. "Food in Iran: The Politics of Insufficiency." In Raymond F. Hopkins et al., eds., *Food, Politics, and Agricultural Development*. Boulder, Col.: Westview Press, 1979, pp. 171-192.

—. *Local Politics and Nation-States: Case Studies in Politics and Policy*. Santa Barbara, Calif.: Clio Press, 1979.

Shahanshahani, Ahmad and Mihssen Kadhim. "Development Problems of an Energy-Based Economy: Iran." *Journal of South Asian and Middle Eastern Studies* 11, 3 (Spring 1979): 57-83.

Skolka, Jiri and Michel Garzuel. *Changes in Income Distribution, Employment, and Structure of the Economy: A Case Study of Iran*. Working paper, Income Distribution and Employment Programme. Geneva: International Labour Office, 1976.

Sorenson, Theodore C. *Kennedy*. London: Hodder & Stoughton, 1965.

Stempel, John. *Inside the Iranian Revolution*. Bloomington: Indiana University Press, 1981.

Strohl, Richard. "Farming Failures: The Fate of Large-Scale Agribusiness in Iran." *Agribusiness Worldwide* (April/May 1980): 12-22.

Tofiq, Firouz. "Development of Iran: A Statistical Note." In Jane W. Jacqz, ed., *Iran: Past, Present and Future*. New York: Aspen Institute for Humanistic Studies, 1976.

—. "Economic Growth and Labour Participation in Iran: A Comment." *Tahqiqat-e Eqtesadi* 7, 18 (Spring 1970): 88-89.

U.N. Industrial Development Organization. *Report on the Evaluation of Selected Activities of the UNIDO: Evaluation Report: Iran*. Vienna: Organization, 1973.

United Nations. *Public Finance Information Papers, Iran*. New York: U.N., 1951.

U.S. Department of Commerce, Domestic and International Business Administration. *Iran: A Survey of U.S. Business Opportunities*. Washington, D.C.: U.S. Government Printing Office, 1977.

U.S. Government Accounting Office. *Audit of the Export-Import Bank of the United States*. Report to Congress by the Comptroller General of the United States. Washington, D.C.: Government Accounting Office, 1972.

Vagar, N. "An Analysis of Iran's Foreign Trade and the Cause of the Stagnation of Its Exports." *Middle East Economic Papers* (December 1969): 89-113.

Vakil, Firouz. "A Development Strategy for Iran: The Role of the Public Sector." Teheran: Plan and Budget Organization, Planometrics and General Economy Bureau, 1976.

—. "Iran's Basic Macroeconomic Problems: A Twenty-Year Horizon." In Jane W. Jacqz, ed., *Iran: Past, Present and Future*. New York: Aspen Institute for Humanistic Studies, 1976.

van Nieuwenhuijze, C.A.O. *Social Stratification and the Middle East: An Interpretation*. Leiden: E.J. Brill, 1965.

Weede, Erich and Horsst Tiefenbach. "Some Recent Explanations of Income Inequality." *International Studies Quarterly* 25, 2 (June 1981): 255-282.

Weinbaum, Marvin G. "Agricultural Policy and Development Politics in Iran." *Middle East Journal* 31, 3 (Summer 1977).

—. *Food, Development, and Politics in the Middle East*. Boulder, Col.: Westview Press, 1982.

World Bank, Statistical Service. *External Medium- and Long-Term Public*

Debt, Past and Projected, 1956-76. Washington, D.C.: International
    Development Agency, 1967.
—. *Trends in Developing Countries, Global Indicators.* Washington, D.C.:
    Bank, 1973.
—. *The World Bank Group in Iran.* Washington, D.C.: Bank, 1968.
—. *World Development Report.* Washington, D.C.: Bank, 1978-83.
—. *World Tables 1976.* Washington, D.C.: Bank, 1976.
Zabih, Sepehr. *The Mossadegh Era: Roots of the Iranian Revolution.* Chicago:
    Liberator Press, 1981.
Zonis, Marvin. *The Political Elite of Iran.* Princeton: Princeton University
    Press, 1971.

SERIALS AND PERIODICALS

AMPO (Japan-Asia quarterly review) (Tokyo)

Aviation Week and Space Technology

Economic Bulletin for Asia and the Pacific

The Economist

Financial Times (London)

Forbes

Interavia Newsletter

Keyhan International (Teheran)

London Times

Merip Reports

The Middle East (Beirut)

Middle East Economic Digest

The Nation

New York Times

Newsweek

Nouvel Observateur

Quarterly Economic Review, Economic Review of Iran (Economist Intelligence Unit)

Washington Post

Index

Index